T0019331

GROWING UP
DUGGAR

From Our Hearts to Yours

Jana, Jill, Jessa, and Jinger Duggar

HOWARD BOOKS
AN IMPRINT OF SIMON & SCHUSTER, INC.
NEW YORK   NASHVILLE   TORONTO   SYDNEY   NEW DELHI

Howard Books
An Imprint of Simon & Schuster, Inc.
1230 Avenue of the Americas
New York, NY 10020

First Howard Books trade paper edition March 2016

HOWARD and colophon are trademarks of Simon & Schuster, Inc.

For information about special discounts for bulk purchases, please contact Simon & Schuster Special Sales at 1-866-506-1949 or business@simonandschuster.com.

The Simon & Schuster Speakers Bureau can bring authors to your live event. For more information or to book an event, contact the Simon & Schuster Speakers Bureau at 1-866-248-3049 or visit our website at www.simonspeakers.com.

Edited by Sue Ann Jones
Additional writing contributed by Charlie Richards and David Waller
Interior design by Davina Mock-Maniscalco

Manufactured in the United States of America

10 9 8 7 6 5 4 3 2

Library of Congress Cataloging-in-Publication Data
Duggar, Jana.
   Growing Up Duggar : it's all about relationships / Jana Duggar, Jill Duggar, Jessa Duggar, Jinger Duggar.
      pages   cm
   1. Duggar, Jana.   2. Duggar, Jill.   3. Duggar, Jessa.   4. Duggar, Jinger.   5. Duggar, Jim Bob—Family.   6. Daughters—United States—Biography.   7. Families—United States—Case studies.   8. Family size—United States—Case studies.   9. Christian life—United States—Case studies.   I. Duggar, Jill.   II. Duggar, Jessa.   III. Duggar, Jinger.   IV. Title.
   HQ536.D85   2014
      306.850973—dc23   2013036030
ISBN 978-1-4516-7920-5
ISBN 978-1-4516-7918-2 (ebook)

ACKNOWLEDGMENTS

WE ARE SO GRATEFUL to all of the following people who have invested their time and energy to make this book a reality:

Charlie Richards, who asked us older girls a lot of questions one day about how our parents have raised us, then insisted that we document our answers in a book to help young ladies and their parents. Charlie also spent a lot of time with us helping us type up and articulate our life experiences to illustrate the principles we live by.

Priscilla and David Waller (Anna Duggar's sister and brother-in-law), who were instrumental in interjecting illustrations and principles that would connect young ladies with practical tips they could apply to everyday life. Anna and Priscilla grew up helping their dad with a prison ministry and have hearts to help young people make right decisions in their lives.

Philis Boultinghouse, with Simon and Schuster, who encouraged us along the way, helped in editing, and was so patient with us throughout this two-year project.

Eileen O'Neill, president of Discovery Communications, who found our family in a *Parents* magazine article ten years ago and asked Bill Hayes and Kirk Streb with Figure 8 Films to contact us about filming our first one-hour documentary. You have enabled us to share our story and God's love with people around the world!

Sue Ann Jones, who received our manuscript while it was still pretty rough and helped us miraculously transform it into what it is. Thank you for your months' worth of work. You did a great job!

Leslie Nunn Reed, our book agent, who contacted our parents several years ago and encouraged them to write down their life story in book form. Because of your vision for our family to share the Bible principles we live by, we have received thousands of e-mails from individuals saying their marriages have been strengthened, relationships with their children have improved, and many families have developed more of a spiritual focus in life.

And to our parents, we love you more than words can say. Thank you for all the sacrifices you have made to have us, provide for us, and point us to a relationship with Jesus. You have guided us through many seas of emotion, encouraging us to trust the Lord no matter what. You are the best parents in the world! You have shown each one of us nineteen kids special love and attention and have spent more time with us individually than many parents do with only one or two children. Thank you for modeling Christ-like living to us and for opening the doors of our home to be a testimony to the world!

Most important, we want to praise our Lord and Savior Jesus Christ. "Soli Deo Gloria!" To God alone be the glory.

Jana, Jill, Jessa & Jinger Duggar

CONTENTS

A Note from the Authors

As we share with you this updated version of the original *Growing Up Duggar*, we also want to share our hearts about the sadness and shock our family experienced in the difficult summer of 2015, which brought the most challenging time we have ever faced. We had long ago forgiven our older brother Josh for his inappropriate actions as a teenager. But when we learned that as an adult in a position of Christian influence he had been unfaithful, we were devastated. The difficulty of the aftermath of this revelation was tremendous, but our faith and trust in God is stronger than ever. Our reliance on His mercy, kindness, and love continues to guide us through every challenge and teaches us that God will work *all* things together for our good (Romans 8:28).

We still believe the principles in this book are as true today as they ever have been. We learn from biblical characters such as David, Moses, Paul, and so many others in the Bible that the failings of an individual or even an entire people can never invalidate the truths of

God's Word. His truth is powerful and effective when we choose to follow it—a choice each one must make personally.

We thank God that you are reading this book and pray that His principles will guide your life. We pray that no matter what comes into your life that your faith will remain strong and that your trust in God will guide you.

"... the eye hath not seen, nor ear heard,
neither have entered into the heart of man,
the things which God hath prepared for them that love Him."
1 Corinthians 2:9

We are so grateful to God for each one of our family members. Here you see us all together in front of an old house, holding our favorite instruments.

GREETINGS

From Our Hearts to Yours

"For I know the thoughts that I think toward you," saith the LORD,
"thoughts of peace, and not of evil, to give you an expected end."
—Jeremiah 29:11

WE'VE WRITTEN THIS BOOK to have the conversation we wish we
could have with each of you one-on-one. The conversation that
may have begun with a letter or an e-mail you wrote to us, or the one
that started with a question you asked or a comment you made after
we spoke to a group somewhere.

Maybe you're that girl we met in the locked ward—we still call it
the cage—in the orphanage in Central America. Jana sat with you there
and shared your hope that someday you would see your mother again.

Maybe you're the single mom whose baby Jill helped deliver as an
apprentice midwife. You smiled and nodded when Jill asked if it would
be okay if she said a prayer for your newborn babe.

You might be the mom who approached Jessa after we spoke at a women's conference somewhere. You asked for ideas about how you could be more helpful and encouraging to your teenage daughter as she struggles with relationships involving boys.

Or perhaps you're the girl Jinger met while she was ministering at the juvenile detention center. You could hardly bring yourself to believe God could really forgive you. But Jinger assured you He can. And will.

Maybe you've never met or contacted us at all, but you've seen our family's show on television, and you're curious.

Whoever you are—whether you're the girl we met who goes to a Christian school and attends church three times a week but is still struggling inside, or the girl with five tattoos and multiple piercings, the one whose parents sent you to the Christian girls retreat Jana works at, hoping you could be "fixed" there—we've written this book to continue the conversation we started with you but couldn't finish because time ran out and we had to go our separate ways. And we've written this book because the volume of letters and e-mails that come to us is more than we can manage individually and because we know how it feels to be curious about something.

We know how weird we must seem to a lot of you, with our different style of dressing and our conservative Christian beliefs. We know it's unusual to be part of a family with nineteen children—one that's featured on reality TV not for the outrageous things we do or say but for the adventures a family the size of ours can have doing ordinary activities.

And we're curious about you, too. We'd like to know how we can impact your life for good. Even though we have never met most of you reading this book, we want you to know we love you and care about your future. We want to share our stories with you, knowing you have a story, too, and hoping something we say here might empower you to use your story, your life, to help others.

RACING AGAINST TIME

SEVERAL YEARS AGO, BEFORE anyone outside our circle of friends and family had ever heard of the Duggars, our parents prayed, "Lord, we pray that our family can impact the world for You!"

Mom and Dad look at life as a race against time. When they prayed that prayer, they were humbly asking God to keep each member of our family on the right track so that we might fulfill the purpose for which He created us, and that He would accomplish as much through us as possible during our time on earth.

At that point, they probably would have been happy if even a single person had become a follower of Jesus because of them. They couldn't have imagined that instead we would be welcomed into millions of homes each week through television (which our family doesn't even watch!). The way that happened is told in their two books, *The Duggars: 20 and Counting* and *A Love That Multiplies*.

Along with our brothers and sisters, we've grown up in the public spotlight (or as we describe it, living in a fishbowl). Now, as adults, we four oldest girls (Jana, twenty-four; Jill, twenty-two; Jessa, twenty-one; and Jinger, twenty) are humbled by the opportunity we've been given to reach out to other girls and young women to share the blessings and lessons we've experienced as we've tried to follow the Christlike way of life we have seen modeled by our parents.

Because so many people, espe-

We've written this book as a way to answer some of the questions we receive in e-mails and letters every day.

cially girls and young women like ourselves, have expressed such curiosity about the way our family works, and because it's just not possible to answer each question individually, we've written this book to tell you about our journey to adulthood, our goals and our faith—and how it all comes together in the work we've chosen to do.

MAKING A DIFFERENCE IN YOUR RELATIONSHIPS

WE DON'T HAVE A perfect family, and we're far from perfect ourselves, but all our lives our parents have encouraged us Duggar kids to have a daily goal of maintaining and strengthening our closest relationships. Those relationships begin with the way we feel about ourselves, accepting the way God created us and seeking His purpose for our lives.

Then we focus on the way we relate to our parents. Our parents have always worked hard to make their relationship with us a priority. They've established family traditions and practices that involve cultivating character and motivating us to maximize our life purpose. And on practical terms, they encourage us to talk with them about not only the small things in life but also deep matters of the heart.

Next, Mom and Dad encourage us kids to be best friends with each other, and so we talk about our relationships with siblings. Throughout our growing-up years Mom and Dad have taught us the importance of maintaining these close relationships, and step by step, they've guided us in how to get along, even though each of us girls now has eighteen siblings—including ten brothers! Of course, as happens in any family, conflicts occur, annoyances are inevitable, and hurt feelings spring up. But Mom and Dad have always taught us to quickly work out those issues so that resentment and bitterness don't creep in and destroy our family's closeness and unity.

Then, we take many of the lessons about getting along with our siblings and apply them to our relationships with friends. Mom and

Dad have taught us the value of choosing our friends carefully and staying true to our own convictions if our friends' behaviors and beliefs veer away from ours.

And then there's the really hot topic we're asked about a lot: *boys.* That's a relationship that is frequently considered by just about every girl we know—including the four oldest Duggar girls! As we write this, we're waiting for the young man God has for us—if marriage is in the future He plans for us. Meanwhile, we've thought a lot about what we want in a future husband and how we anticipate courtship will happen. As you might expect, it's pretty different from the way many couples interact these days. For one thing, it may surprise you to know it doesn't involve typical dating, but what we call courtship—or "dating with a purpose."

Beyond our relationships with ourselves, our parents, our siblings, our friends, and boys, we also discuss our relationships with our culture, our country, and the world at large. As Christians, we believe that we are to be "in" the world but not "of" the world, as the Bible says; so we talk about how we relate to the Internet, movies, entertainment, and music. Then we'll share our passion for being involved in the political realm and how we want to make a difference there, as well as our commitment and desire to reach out to people in faraway countries, showing Jesus's love to people we don't even know. The Bible teaches us to put others' needs above our own and to treat other people the way we want to be treated. We call it having a ministry mindset, and it's something that's stressed in the Duggar home. We'll tell you how that emphasis has led us to pursue the work we're doing now.

Though the topics and stories will vary from chapter to chapter, the theme of this whole book is *relationships;* and the foundation for *all* our relationships with people—as well as our relationship with our culture, country, and the world—is our relationship with God. We don't have a separate chapter on our relationship with God, but our message about that is woven throughout every chapter and topic of the book. We hope that as you read this book, you'll gain a clear understanding of how *everything* we do is rooted in our faith in Him.

You'll see that the length of the chapters in this book varies a bit—but every chapter is divided into short, easy-to-read segments. You can read as much or as little at one sitting as you like—whatever works for you. We have written this book with *you* in mind.

Most important, we hope this book will inspire you to let the love of God and His Son Jesus Christ empower you to make a difference through the relationships that fill your own life.

We may have met some of you when we were speaking
(and laughing) at a conference somewhere.

Growing Up
Duggar

1

YOUR RELATIONSHIP WITH YOURSELF

Getting to know and love the girl in the mirror

I will praise Thee;
for I am fearfully and wonderfully made.
—Psalms 139:14

WHEN OUR PARENTS WERE planning to build our current house in northwest Arkansas, they asked us kids how many bedrooms we thought the house should have. It was an easy question for us to answer: we wanted to be together. So, upstairs in our house today, there's one big room for all the girls, one big room for all the boys, and our parents' bedroom with an adjoining nursery.

Jana and I (Jill) sleep in double beds with our youngest sisters, Jordyn and Josie, and the other girls sleep in twin- or youth-sized beds. It's always an exciting time when the littlest sister gets to move from the nursery to the "big girls' room" with us, although they're always free to toddle back to Mom and Dad's room if they need to. We love the late-night conversations and falling asleep each night surrounded by our sisters.

One night a few years ago as I was putting my retainer in my mouth at bedtime, my sister Johannah, then probably five or six, asked what it was. I told her it was something I slept with to help keep my teeth aligned now that I didn't have to wear braces anymore.

"Can I wear it?" Johannah asked.

We Duggars do love to share a lot of things but, thankfully, dental appliances aren't among them. I smiled and told her no, it was made just for me and it wouldn't fit her mouth at all.

Thinking about that conversation later reminded me that we can't conform ourselves to other people's molds. But we try sometimes, don't we? It's inevitable that human beings, particularly teenagers and *especially* teenage girls, go through times when they may try to remake themselves into something, or someone, they're not. Every girl has a tendency to compare herself to other girls, noticing how they dress or style their hair, how much they weigh, how they talk, the words and phrases they use, and how guys respond to them.

You may think that kids like the Duggars, who are homeschooled and don't watch TV or read secular magazines, are immune from feelings like that, but we're not! We've experienced some of those same negative feelings about the girl in the mirror that you may be feeling right now or have felt in the past.

Jinger didn't seem to mind when we visited a dude ranch and deputies Jessa, left, and Jill took her into custody.

All of us have gone through times when we've felt we needed to lose weight. And we've all looked at the girl in the mirror and sometimes found things that just didn't seem to measure up.

Are you going through a time in your life when you're being critical of the girl in *your* mirror?

ACCEPTING THE GIRL IN THE MIRROR

THAT'S HARD, ISN'T IT? You've looked at that girl in the mirror all your life and had made friends with her, and then one day you look at her and notice the blemish on her forehead or the nose that isn't as cute as your friend's nose. Maybe the girl who seemed just fine yesterday now seems too short or too tall, too thin or too heavy. Maybe her clothes, the ones that were your favorites yesterday, seem completely wrong today. And that hair. It's ridiculous!

Suddenly the girl who looked just fine yesterday seems like a total loser today compared to those cute girls at the mall . . . or your school . . . or your homeschool group . . . or even your church.

So then what happens? You reject that girl in the mirror, and in your heart you worry that she'll be rejected by others, too, including those you admire. Fear of rejection is one of the major problems facing teenagers and young adults today. It affects almost all of us, including the Duggar kids, at one time or another.

For example, I (Jill) can remember a Sunday morning when we were getting ready for church and I went through multiple outfit changes because I was trying to measure up. The night before, I had stood in our closet for at least ten minutes trying to decide what I would wear the next day. (Ever been there?)

Finally I chose an outfit I thought was suitable. I took it upstairs and laid it out so it would be ready the next morning. But when I walked out of the bathroom Sunday morning, dressed and ready to go, I noticed how great Jessa looked wearing an adorable outfit she had recently found at a thrift store. Plus, she had the cutest aviator sunglasses perched on her head and a stylish leather bag slung over her shoulder. Suddenly the outfit I had chosen for myself the night before seemed totally wrong. I wanted to look as cute as Jessa did.

So I hurried back downstairs to the closet and stood there for what seemed like another ten minutes, trying to find something to wear. Then I heard Dad's voice over the intercom saying, "Everyone hurry up! It's nine forty, and the first vanload is leaving for church."

I grabbed a skirt off the rack and tried it on, but then I remembered that the shirt I usually wear with it was dirty. I hurriedly put that choice back on the hanger and found a cute denim skirt—only to realize the zipper was broken. I was growing more frustrated and about to settle for the original outfit I had put on that morning when my eye landed on a brown-striped skirt. *Perfect*, I thought. *Why didn't I think of this in the first place?*

But then I had to change my shoes to go with the skirt, and—or where *were* those sandals that looked so great with this skirt? I finally rushed out of the clothes closet and around the corner to the bathroom mirror. Oops! With all the changing, my hair had gotten messed up. I hurriedly worked to restore order to it and then discovered we had run out of hair spray in that bathroom. Running to

While we sometimes do the shopping for our family at warehouse stores, our favorite place to shop for clothes is thrift stores.

another bathroom to grab some, I could hear the car horn honking as the second load of churchgoers waited for me.

It was nearly ten o'clock—church time—as I rushed out the door. Not exactly the way one would want to prepare for a morning of worshipping our Creator! And it all started because I compared myself to one of my sisters and felt that my appearance fell short.

It seems like such a trivial matter now, looking back on that morning, but it's so typical of teenagers, especially young ladies. It's easy for us to compare ourselves to others and think we have to be like them to measure up or to be accepted. But too often it's impossible to meet the goals of perfection we set for ourselves, and as a result, we end up dealing with all sorts of destructive feelings: poor self-worth, lack of confidence, jealousy, discontentment, and so much more. Before we know it, momentary concerns about our outward appearance turn into lies about ourselves that swirl constantly through our minds, telling us, "I'm not good enough." "I'm a failure." "Nobody loves me."

Ultimately, we lose sight of what's most important: our inward character.

GIVING POWER TO OTHERS

FOR MANY YEARS, I (Jessa) couldn't care less about what I wore and how I looked. I was the typical happy little Duggar kid, filling my day with homeschool work and playing with my siblings and friends.

But life changed for me when I was about twelve or thirteen. Whenever I was around friends outside our family, I became very quiet and self-conscious—really insecure about the way I looked, dressed, and acted.

I had friends who were really beautiful, and whenever we were together I compared myself to them and always came up lacking something. These critical feelings caused me to have a mistaken view of my friends *and* myself—thinking they were perfect and I wasn't. I felt so ashamed and awkward that I couldn't even talk to anyone about my feelings. I felt overwhelmed and stuck in that negative mind-set.

I remember during that stage of my life having mixed feelings when I was invited to a friend's birthday party. I was eager to go to the party but overly concerned that I had to look and act just right. What a dilemma, worrying about what clothes I would wear, what I would say, what gift I would bring!

I can still feel those butterflies fluttering in my stomach as we drove up to the birthday girl's big yellow house. I was excited but nervous at the same time. I was thinking about all the conversations I'd had with the girl and our friends that focused on outward appearance—who had cute clothes and who didn't, whose hairstyle we wanted to copy and whose hair was always a wreck. The butterflies continued to churn as I arrived at the front door with another guest.

Our younger sister Joy is beautiful inside and out.

"Oh, I *love* your outfit!" the birthday girl said to the friend beside me.

She didn't say anything about what I was wearing, so I immediately assumed she didn't think my outfit was as perfect as the other girl's.

Soon the party was under way, and I enjoyed all the games, but after we'd sung "Happy Birthday" and settled around the living room for cake and ice cream, the topic of movies came up. I hadn't seen the popular movie the other girls were talking about, and I felt out of place. The critical thoughts came bubbling back up: *Jessa, you don't fit in. It's obvious you're not as cool as the other girls.*

Looking back, I can see how my inward struggles grew worse because I craved the birthday girl's approval—as did several others in this group of friends. I wanted her to like me. Receiving her approval made me feel good about myself. But when she let me know, or when I assumed, that she didn't quite approve of my appearance or something I said or did (or didn't do), I felt worse about myself. I felt as though I had failed—and I carried those feelings with me for days after we'd been together.

My friend seemed to be the perfect picture of the girl I was not. She was tall with beautiful hair and big, brown eyes. She was slender and attractive. After being with this girl, I would look in the mirror and see frizzy hair, ordinary eyes, and a body that wasn't as slender or as beautiful as hers. Constantly comparing myself to her was the perfect recipe for jealousy and discontentment.

ACCEPTING THE UNCHANGEABLES

WHAT POWER I WAS giving my friend by allowing her to make me feel that way about the girl in the mirror! The same girl who all my life had smiled back at me each day and been an accepted and essential part of me now became someone I looked at with a constantly critical eye.

Thankfully, about that time, I heard a Bible teacher share an inspiring message about how God has perfectly designed each one of us with ten aspects of life that, without extraordinary action, we cannot change and that He wants us to accept:

1. Who our parents are
2. Who our siblings are
3. The order in which we are born into our family (oldest or youngest, etc.)
4. Our nationality
5. Whether we're a girl or boy
6. Our mental capacity
7. The time we were born in history
8. Our physical features
9. The natural aging process
10. The date we will die

This teacher said that if we reject our physical features, we reject our self-image and often assume that others will reject us, too. This assumption can cause us to make poor decisions based on our own misperception of ourselves.

That's right where I was in my relationship with my "powerful" friend. I realized I had been ungrateful to God for the wonderful way He had made me. I had pushed aside what the Bible tells us—that God looks on each one of us as His uniquely beautiful creation—and instead I let an immature teenage girl make me feel bad about myself.

When my parents realized what was happening, they wisely helped me rethink the priority I had put on this friendship, and they encouraged me to ask God to forgive me for not appreciating the way He had created me. Looking back, I feel sad to think what it must have been like for God to see me, His unique and carefully designed Jessa, looking in the mirror and disliking the girl He'd created with such love.

Have you been there? Standing in front of a mirror with a negative attitude about the girl you're seeing? You're not alone! All of us, including the Duggar girls, have had times when we compare ourselves with the way other girls dress, do their hair, how much they weigh, how they carry themselves, and how guys respond to them.

But if we're upset with that girl in the mirror, it means we're upset with God for how He designed us. We may start to think He messed up when He de-signed us or even that He doesn't love us. And that leads us to put our confidence and trust in someone else—such as a teenage peer who somehow gains a more powerful influence on our lives than God.

Jill, left, and Jessa followed the traditional custom of taking a "mud bath" while visiting the Dead Sea in Israel.

If that's where you are right now, we're here to help you see yourself through new eyes—God's powerful, love-filled, encouraging, and forgiving eyes. We hope to convince you that God loves you more than anyone else in the world loves you and that He has a unique plan for your life. We've learned through firsthand experience that when we make *Him* the priority in our lives and seek *His* way and *His* approval, He will fill us with a humble confidence that gives us inward strength and makes us immune to the sometimes-harsh judgment of others who don't have our best interests at heart.

Our parents worked hard to instill that idea within us as we were growing up.

HONORING HOW GOD MADE YOU

ULTIMATELY, HOW WE CARE for ourselves (hair, makeup, clothes) tells others what we think about the way God made us. So our primary goal is to honor the Lord with our appearance. A friend of ours said it this way: "A girl's outward appearance should send a message that says, 'This is who I am,' not 'This is what I do.'" We want to maintain this perspective and keep our focus on pointing others to God.

Accepting the way God has uniquely made us helps us not to be so concerned with how others view us. Many people have demonstrated that truth to us. One of them was a sweet, Christian woman I (Jill) met last year when we were on a trip out west. She invited us to her home for dinner one evening, and while we were there, she and her husband showed us around their place and told us a little about themselves.

She shared that she came from an Italian family, and then she joked that a lot of Italians have long noses. She said when she was about to graduate from high school her mom came to her with a check that was a gift for her to be able to get surgery done to make her nose smaller.

The woman told us she was taken by surprise—and so was her mom when the daughter told her she wouldn't be carrying on the family's "nose job" tradition. "I'm content with the way God made me," she said.

That conversation really made an impact on all of us girls, reminding us that none of us can choose the design God selected for us when He created us, but we *can* choose how we respond to His design. Contentment is realizing that God has provided everything we need for our present happiness.

Another key is recognizing the "unchangeable" things in our life and choosing to live joyfully with them. For this lady, it was accepting her Italian nose. For us it may be our ears, height, shoe size, gender, parents, siblings, or any number of other things.

Sure, it's technically possible to change some of these things. You can renounce your citizenship and pledge your loyalty to another country, and you can have surgery to change some of your physical features, but before you do, we hope you'll carefully and prayerfully consider what God originally gave you when He created you. If you go through life comparing yourself to others, you can always find someone who is smarter, better-looking—whatever—and it's easy to become discontent, depressed, or even angry at God.

But if we choose to be grateful and thank God for the unchangeable things in our lives, whether it is facial features or a birthmark we were born with—or even physical scars that have come about later in life from accidents such as burns or being injured in a car wreck—it changes our whole perspective on life. We will finally be able to overcome fear of rejection and live confidently and contentedly with these unchangeable things that we did not choose for ourselves.

IMPROVING THE CHANGEABLES

NOW, SOMETIMES THERE ARE changeable things in life that can use improvement—our weight, for instance. When we were younger, most of us could eat about anything we wanted to and not gain weight, but those times have changed. We've found that most of us older Duggars have a tendency to gain weight.

Over the years, Mom has done her best to prepare nutritious meals for us, and she has always kept healthy fruits

We might not be the neatest sushi makers, but Jana, Josie, Jedidiah, and Jackson sure had fun trying when we visited the Japanese Sushi Academy.

and vegetables around for us to snack on throughout the day, whether they are grown in our own garden or purchased from the local farmers market. We have chosen to avoid pork, and instead we choose grass-fed beef or lean poultry. While we do eat some processed foods, we try to be selective, and we do not keep a stash of sodas, potato chips, or Pop-Tarts around the house.

And the Duggar children are very active, whether we're building a tree fort or playing our favorite sports together—some of which include basketball, kickball, football, foursquare, and volleyball (and we have enough players to make up at least two teams!). But just the same, we have found that as we grow older, it can be challenging to stay fit and in shape.

Mom told us she put on nearly forty pounds a few years ago throughout the course of several pregnancies. She tried several weight-loss programs but began to think she would never be able to slim back down. Finally she tried Weight Watchers and learned about making wiser food choices. During one of the weekly meetings the leader said, "When it comes to losing weight, it's really eighty percent diet and twenty percent exercise. You can eat more calories in a few minutes than you can burn off in an hour-long workout."

Weight Watchers taught Mom about portion control, and it provided a great accountability system. She also started exercising three miles a day on an elliptical machine. By working to keep in shape, she looks and feels great, and she's been a big inspiration to the rest of us!

A couple of other changeable things in life are makeup and hair. We heard a pastor say one time, "Any ol' barn looks better with some paint on it!" Our goal when we wear makeup is to look natural, so no wild colors and it's not painted on an inch thick. But cosmetics can help cover blemishes, accent natural beauty, and draw attention to your *countenance* (another word for your face).

It's the same with hair. When cared for properly and thoughtfully styled, it too can be a beautiful frame to draw attention to your countenance.

We Duggar girls choose to wear our hair rather long, but we could wear shorter styles if we wanted to. Our hairstyle is our choice, and we choose longer hair based on our understanding of 1 Corinthians 11:14–15. It says that, while it is a shame for a man to have long hair, a woman's hair is her glory. We figure, if God says our hair is our "glory," then He must have considered it a gift to us, and we want to take care of it and put a little effort each day into styling it.

Twenty-five Duggars plus our cousin Amy, Grandma, and our film crew traveled together to London, where the girls took time out from sightseeing for a photo in front of Buckingham Palace.

But if we become obsessed with having the *perfect* hairstyle and spend two hours in front of the mirror every morning making sure every hair is in place, that's going a little too far. (And it would also be nearly impossible in the Duggar household, given the limited number of bathrooms and the seemingly unlimited number of people needing to use them at any given time!)

One thing we're trying to do in this book is to share not only what we've been taught but also what we've learned through firsthand experience. I (Jana) can tell you I learned an important lesson about hair—and also about making rash decisions.

One day several years ago when I was a young teenager, some of us girls were talking with a friend and she mentioned something about how you could put highlights in your hair by simply using peroxide or lemon juice. It was certainly inexpensive and sounded easy to do, so I decided to try it. I wasn't making a big change to my sandy-brown hair, just adding some highlights, so I didn't consider it a big deal and didn't ask Mama about it—and didn't mention my plan to anyone else. I didn't know exactly how to do it, but I was sure I could figure it out. I mean, how hard could it be to put one simple liquid on my hair?

So, a few days later, I got some peroxide and put a rather generous amount on my hair, dabbing it on and then combing it through. I stood there looking in the mirror, not seeing any change, and thinking, *Hmmm. I guess it didn't work.*

Oh well. It was a nice, sunshiny day, and I decided to do some work in the flower beds, something I enjoy.

A few hours later, I came back inside and couldn't believe what I saw in the mirror! Everyone else was surprised, too. My twin brother, John-David, said, "Wow, Jana! Did you dye your hair orange?"

When Dad saw it and I explained what I'd done, he said, "Oh, Jana, peroxide isn't something to mess around with. I wish you had talked to Mom about it first!"

By that time, I was wishing the same thing! I told Dad, "I didn't think it would bleach my hair *this* much."

It was hard living with the prolonged consequences of my spur-of-the-minute decision. Then, as my hair began to grow out, it was no longer just orange but two-toned orange and brown. I was so embarrassed by it that, once again, I acted impulsively. I went to a beauty supply store and asked the salesclerk what she recommended. She suggested I cover up the problem by using a slightly darker shade of hair color than my natural shade.

I was so determined to fix the problem that I ended up picking a color that was too dark, leaving me with nearly jet-black hair—and teaching me an important life lesson. Since then I've been content with the color God chose for my hair.

We're not saying there's anything wrong with dyeing your hair (although we recommend that you know what you're doing before you try it!). We love to experiment with different styles, and some of us may decide someday to add highlights or change our hair color. But most likely, it won't be Jana!

Like many people—maybe like *you*—we sometimes feel we need to make a change in our appearance or in some other aspect of our lives, but we're learning that it's wise to ask advice, and we certainly need to pray about it. We like to look our best, but we don't want to get carried away and let a focus on outward beauty cause us to lose sight of what's most important: developing inward character.

CHOOSING OUR FAVORITE STYLES

NOW, LET US TAKE a moment to chat about the Duggar girls' fashion preferences and shopping habits. What we're about to share are our personal standards—not everyone shares the same convictions. Even families who share our Christian values may not share our same convictions about modesty. Daddy reminds us regularly that if the Lord shows *you* something from Scripture, then you have a responsibility to respond to that guidance. We simply honor what God wants our family to do. It doesn't mean that what we do is for everybody. God convicts different people of different things at different times.

As we were growing up, Mom and Dad always explained in detail why we do what we do and that everything had a root in Scripture. Now that we're older, we do our own research. Dad and Mom desire each one of us to *individually* follow God.

Duggars tend to be night owls instead of early risers, but quite a few times we have had to get up super early to gather in our home's living room for remote broadcasts for the *Today* show.

Throughout our younger years, Dad taught us all to be frugal, and Mom did an amazing job of clothing her big family well on a shoestring budget—and thrift store purchases. Her focus was never on whether her children were dressed in the most expensive clothing but on who filled our hearts.

We're aware of modern fashion trends because we travel a lot and interact with a wide variety of people. But we prefer to wear modest and feminine skirts and dresses; it's how Mom dressed us as we were growing up; and now that we are older, it's what we choose for ourselves. It's our own personal conviction based on scriptures such as

Deuteronomy 22:5 and 1 Timothy 2:9. And since our favorite shopping style is *frugality,* our favorite places to shop are thrift and consignment stores. If you shop there enough (and we go fairly often!) you can find great clothes at great prices.

While some people shop in used clothing stores begrudgingly, we absolutely love it! Many times you can find adorable outfits for about 80 to 90 percent off the prices you might pay for them at the mall. It's like a treasure hunt! When we're traveling, as we get close to the place we're going to stay, we girls get online and start mapping out nearby thrift stores.

Duggars simply love deals. Mom and Dad continuously teach us to "buy used and save the difference," and we enjoy both the shopping and the savings.

We aren't especially interested in labels, except maybe for those brands we know are well made and won't fall apart in the laundry. We simply want to dress in a way that is modest and cute. We want to be respectful of those around us, and we don't want those we meet and work with to be distracted by what we're wearing.

It's okay to enhance or accent whatever beauty God has given us, but we try to be careful not to wear clothes that are too tight and draw attention to the wrong places. But this does not mean we go out dressing frumpy or trying to look formless. Clothing can be cute, trendy, and stylish, and still entirely modest.

We do not dress modestly because we are ashamed of the body God has given us; quite the contrary. We realize that our body is a special gift from God and that He intends for it to be shared only with our future husband (Proverbs 5:18–20). For this reason, we avoid low-cut, cleavage-showing, gaping, or bare-shouldered tops; and when needed, we wear an undershirt. We try to make it a habit to always cover the top of our shirt with our hand when we bend over. We don't want to play the peekaboo game with our neckline.

Scripture states in several places that the uncovering of the thigh is *nakedness,* so we have also chosen not to wear short skirts; our goal is to wear skirts that come below the knee.

It just makes sense that convictions should carry over into every area of life, so looking ahead, we each desire to maintain this standard of modesty when choosing our wedding dress. For us, this will mean finding a dress with sleeves and a modest neckline. We feel that many designers encourage girls to flaunt things to all their wedding guests that should be seen only by their groom. However, there are bridal companies who understand that it is possible to make wedding gowns absolutely gorgeous while being entirely modest. Several of our friends have purchased stunning dresses from designers such as www.beautifully modest.com or www .totallymodest.com.

Everybody makes mistakes. Toddler Jana realized she'd made one when she pulled a long strand of toilet tissue off the roll—and then couldn't figure out how to get it back on.

It is our goal to maintain modesty when we are swimming or participating in other activities as well. While long shorts and a swim shirt have worked in the past, we have now found many modest swimwear companies online that make cute styles that are both practical and comfortable for swimming. (One that we have used is wholesomewear.com.)

Mom says that after she became a Christian, she realized, *I wouldn't go out in public wearing just my bra and panties, but how is wearing a bikini or even a one-piece at the pool or beach any different than that?* She felt convicted that there wasn't any difference.

It's true that boys need to keep their minds out of the gutter, but we girls also have a responsibility not to dress or act in a way that builds up sensual desires in guys.

As Christians, it is our hope that through the way we dress, act, and carry ourselves, others will be able to see God's love shining through our faces, our words, and our actions. That's the "clothing label" we want to wear.

As teenagers we may have gone through times when we were insecure and momentarily influenced by the world around us instead of by the God who made us. But through our parents' prayers, and ultimately by God's grace, God has brought us back to what's really important. The stories of how that happened are what we hope to share with you in the following pages.

2

YOUR RELATIONSHIP WITH YOUR PARENTS

Love, respect, and communication

Honour thy father and thy mother:
that thy days may be long.
—Exodus 20:12

WE GET A LOT of letters and e-mails from girls who watch *19 Kids and Counting,* and many of them ask our advice on tough issues. We don't pretend to have all the answers to the difficult situations some of these girls are going through. But, in this book, we want to share what we've learned and what we've experienced that might relate to their questions.

Most important, we pray for the girls who share their hearts with us.

A lot of the girls have written to us about the pain caused by their dad abandoning their family or their parents getting a divorce. Others are still living all under the same roof, but there is much strife, contention, and anger.

Our dad has shared that when he was growing up, his dad did not have a spiritual focus, and because of that his father often did not have the right attitudes and responses. This caused a lot of problems in his family. They struggled financially and had the utilities temporarily shut off many times. At one point their house was foreclosed on.

But his mother was a strong woman of faith who consistently encouraged Dad and his older sister to trust the Lord no matter what came their way. Dad said he tried to pick out his dad's good qualities and apply them to his life—things like sales ability and a giving heart—but leave out the bad qualities. He also looked up to other godly men in his church as role models. Romans 8:28 became Dad's life verse: "And we know that all things work together for good to them that love God, to them who are the called according to His purpose."

This means that as we trust God, He will work all situations to turn out for eventual good in our lives. So instead of getting angry and upset when things don't go our way, we need to thank God and look for the benefits that can come from the situation. He has promised that even the seemingly bad will work out for our good!

As a result of Dad's childhood, one obvious benefit was that he gained great faith in God. There were a few times when his family honestly didn't know where their next meal would come from, but his mom would encourage them to pray, and he saw God answer their prayers countless times. This caused him to develop a spiritual focus at a young age. Also, with his father not striving to be a spiritual leader in his life, Dad determined early on that, by God's grace, he would become a godly husband and father to his own family one day.

Dad's background has also given him sensitivity toward others who have grown up in similar situations. Our parents have led our family to reach out to those around us who for one reason or another don't have a mom or dad. As we have reached out, we have truly felt that we have received the greater blessing in return through the love others have shown us.

Mom's dad spent most of his growing-up years in an orphanage. Despite that rough beginning, he chose not to go through life feeling sorry for himself or to wallow in depression but rather to live cheerfully and encourage those around him. He became a very tender-hearted man and a hard worker. He got promoted into management at a large machine shop and eventually took a job that moved his family from Cincinnati, Ohio, to Springdale, Arkansas, when Mom was four years old. He determined to become a loving father, and he and his wife ended up having seven children (our mom is the seventh).

This goes to show that no matter what kind of family situation you grow up in, God can use it to make you stronger. And as you resolve to develop a genuine love and servant's heart toward your family, you will see God begin to work in their hearts as well.

BOUNDARIES

SOME PARENTS ARE A little on the strict side; others are more laid-back. But it is important for each of us to realize that our parents love us. Even though parents make mistakes and are not perfect, it's important that we honor and respect them.

As we get older and show signs of maturity, we gain more freedoms, but with greater freedom comes greater responsibility. For years, our parents have invested in our lives and mentored us with the goal of sending us out into this world to make a difference.

We have received letters from girls whose parents want to be "cool," so they avoid telling their kids *no*. Those parents probably assume their teenagers are mature enough to set their own appropriate boundaries and make wise choices. But we know from our own experience that young teenagers often *don't* have the maturity needed for making decisions, especially for deciding issues that can carry life-long impact. We made plenty of poor decisions as teenagers, and while we're thankful our parents gave us increasing freedom to decide tough issues for ourselves as we matured, we're also grateful they didn't just turn us loose to decide *everything* independently as soon as we turned thirteen—or even eighteen!

Instead, they have given us plenty of guidance and have provided a solid foundation during our growing-up years. When each of us children learned to read, they encouraged us to read and study the Bible, and as we grew they encouraged us to start thinking about the convictions and guidelines God would have us set for ourselves. In this chapter we're going to talk about how they did that.

THE HOTTEST HOT TOPIC

ONE OF THE BIGGEST issues teenage girls focus on is boys—in particular, one boy. At least that's what girls tell us in letters that usually say something like "There's this boy . . ."

We get the feeling that the world thinks strained relationships between teenage girls and their parents occur most often because the girl wants to date a certain boy and the parents say no. Usually it's because the girl is too young or because the boy isn't "good enough" for their daughter. And certainly we get letters from girls (and parents) in those situations, so we know that's often the case.

But we have also received several letters from girls who wished their parents would have provided

Duggars grow up sharing lots of hugs, laughter, and love. From left: Jinger, Jana, Jill, and Jessa.

more boundaries for them when they were dating. Surprising, but true.

Before we go any further, we need to clarify that none of us girls actually plans to date (as most people would define dating). If marriage is in God's future plan for any of us, we desire for our relationships with our future husbands to develop through *courtship*, rather than today's norm of dating. We'll talk more about that in chapter 5, but for now we want to focus on a teenage girl's relationship with her parents as she becomes aware of teenage boys and starts thinking about dating or courtship.

Here's the bottom line: The relationship a girl has with her dad often influences how she will relate to boys. Girls want to believe their dads love them and will protect them. When they don't feel that, they often go searching for those things from guys. This can lead to unwise decisions, which in turn bring a host of consequences and painful memories.

One young woman who wrote to us desperately wanted her father to at least check out the boys who wanted to date her. But he didn't. When a boy came to pick her up at her home, her dad would send her on her way with the words "Have a good time."

Maybe that seems like every teenage girl's dream—a dad who lets her do whatever she wants or go out with any guy she wants to date. But when we reached out to mentor this girl, she told us that as she and the boy-of-the-week would drive away, she might have been smiling on the outside, but inside she felt empty. Worthless. Not even important enough for her father to bother checking out the boy who was taking her out.

Children grow up seeing what their parents value. We are grateful to have parents whose faith in Jesus is their top priority. They value their relationship with Him, and second to that, they cherish their relationship with each other and with their family. A girl watches what her father takes care of: his sports car, his custom-made golf clubs, his investments. It's unlikely that a dad would entrust his prized convertible to a teenage boy he didn't really know and just let the kid take it out for a spin without supervision; but that same dad may let a relatively unknown boy drive off with his daughter without giving it much thought.

That dad may think he's being a great, understanding father who wants to make his daughter happy. But instead he may be striking a severe blow to that daughter's self-esteem. It's easy for her, in that situation, to think she's not good enough, not important enough, to be loved. And that kind of thinking can make her vulnerable to the first boy who tells her he loves her and wants to share that love through a physical relationship.

The girl may so yearn to feel valued and accepted by a male that she gives in to the boy's desires. But too often the boy's "love" for her turns out to be fleeting, and the girl is left feeling cast off and degraded. From there, things can easily spiral downward as the girl's yearning to feel valued intensifies and she seeks acceptance from the next boy who comes along. We hear from a lot of girls in this painful situation.

Girls want their dad to be their protector. They want to feel valued by their dad more than any possession he owns. If he doesn't show that he values her, daughters can easily feel devalued, even betrayed.

If you're a girl in this situation, we know it's unlikely that you'll go to your father and say, "Dad, I'd like you to be stricter with me when it comes to dating." But we en-

Even though there are a lot of birthdays to celebrate in our family, our parents make each of them special. Here Jinger, left, Jessa, and Dad admire the cake Mom made to celebrate Jessa's seventh birthday.

courage you to pray about your relationship with your dad and ask God to give him those characteristics he's missing, or to give him insights that will help improve his relationship with you. And then do *your* part: show respect when your dad makes hard decisions; don't argue or pout when he sets guidelines for your family. And watch for opportunities to spend time with your dad and talk with him, knowing that close communication can strengthen your relationship.

The Importance of Love and Respect

Of course, sometimes things happen in families that make communication difficult, if not impossible. We hear from girls whose families struggle with a wide range of challenges in their parents: alcoholism, drug addiction, physical abuse, or the absence of a parent due to death or divorce. We're barely more than teens ourselves, and in these situations we don't have the professional training to give these girls the kind of emergency assistance they need. So in those cases, we urge girls to reach out to a trusted adult—the other parent, a pastor or pastor's wife, a Sunday school teacher, or Christian counselor. Meanwhile we can pray for their safety and emotional well-being, and we can offer a listening ear as they pour out the cries of their hearts.

When safety isn't an issue and communication is broken, we share what we know about healing the rift. Again, we're certainly not experts in family counseling, but we've grown up in a family that strives to make good, honest communication a top priority, and we're glad to share some things we've learned over the years if it can be of help.

An opportunity to do that came not too long ago when one of my (Jill's) friends called me with the devastating news that her dad was leaving the family, and her parents were getting a divorce. We cried together as she sobbed out her heartache. She has given me permission to share her story in hopes that it can benefit others in similar situations.

As one of the older children in her family, she felt a huge responsibility to set an example of loving encouragement for her younger siblings, but that seemed impossible when she was battling so many emotions herself. When she tried to talk with her dad about his leaving and tell him how hurt she and her siblings were, the conversation ended with both of them exploding in anger. She and her dad both said things they probably wished they hadn't said.

As days turned into weeks and then months, we continued to talk frequently, but it didn't seem that her relationship with her dad could ever be reconciled. Each time we talked, I told her I would be praying for her—and particularly for her relationship with her father. But it seemed that she and her dad were growing further apart.

When the divorce was finalized, it included mandatory visitation for the dad with all the children. But because of the strained relationship between my friend and her father, he said he wouldn't force her to come. "It's up to you," he told her.

Maybe her dad meant well by not forcing her, but his words hurt her deeply. By leaving it up to her, her dad seemed to be saying he didn't care about his daughter—at least that's how it felt to her.

On the outside, my friend seemed tough and acted like it didn't hurt, but on the inside she was heartbroken, and often when we talked by phone, the tears came pouring out. Despite the pain, she knew her relationship with her father was important. And she knew in her heart that her dad felt the same way. They just didn't seem to know how to get past all the hurt.

Then, out of the blue, months after their big blowup when he left the family, the girl's dad invited her and her siblings to go to a ball game with him. But again, he let her know she didn't have to go if she didn't want to.

My friend and I talked about her dad's invitation, and she acknowledged that it meant her dad was still trying to have a relationship with her. He hadn't given up, even though it seemed like he didn't care.

The girl decided to go, even though her heart was still full of so much pain and bitterness toward her dad that she was afraid it would come rushing out and damage their relationship even more. But the truth was, she missed her dad and longed to spend time doing fun things with him the way they'd done before the divorce.

When she asked for my advice on how to handle this situation with her dad, I told her I didn't know what it was like to be in a family split by divorce, but I know the feeling of wanting to have healthy family relationships.

I encouraged the girl to honor her dad because, despite her hurt feelings, he is still her father. Everyone wants to be respected, but it's especially important for fathers. I suggested that to begin improving their relationship, the first thing she needed to work on was being positive. If she felt like she was going to say something critical or negative, I advised her that it would be better, at least for now, to choose not to say anything. Along with this goal, I encouraged her to pray for her dad and ask God to help him have more patience and kindness and to pray that he would be "slow to anger," a phrase that occurs several times in the Bible describing a characteristic of God.

The Bible teaches that whenever we encounter those who are troubled by harmful character qualities—things like anger, dishonesty, impatience, vanity—we should pray that God will help them to develop the opposite quality—things like a peaceful demeanor, truthfulness, patience, and humility. I shared these suggestions with the girl, and we prayed together that God would help her dad replace his negative character qualities with positive ones. We also asked God to do the same thing for the girl, replacing her anger with respect and courtesy.

So they went to the ball game, and she called me afterward, excitedly describing the outing with her dad. Things had been a little strained at first, she said, but the afternoon had passed peacefully, and there had even been moments of fun and laughter. She felt they'd taken a solid step toward restoring their relationship.

Our travel schedule makes it hard to have pets, so we're grateful to neighbors who share their friendly animals, and as you can see from the smile on Jana's face here, we did enjoy having a horse named Samson several years ago.

I suggested that a good next step would be for her to find something she could praise her dad for or thank him for. The next time they were together, she thanked him for reaching out to her, and she told him, "I like it when you call to talk to me."

As she has kept her focus on honoring her father and looking for ways to be positive and praise him, their communication has gotten better. And although the situation is still challenging, by demonstrating an attitude of love and respect she's helping their relationship improve.

If you're going through a tough time and your relationship with one or both of your parents is strained, we hope you'll ask God to give you the wisdom and the courage to do your part in making a difference. Show love and respect. Look for opportunities to express gratefulness for the sacrifices they make as parents, and avoid being critical. Pray that God will replace the negative character qualities in both you and your parent with the opposite character traits and then watch for times when you can put those qualities to work.

CRUCIAL COMMUNICATION

LOVE AND RESPECT ARE important in our family—and in every family. But those qualities don't always come about automatically. When you see the Duggar family on television happily having adventures at home and around the country, it may seem like we never have disagreements or that we kids never get upset with each other or with Mom or Dad. But we're human. Sometimes siblings irritate us! We get our feelings hurt! We get disappointed when things don't turn out the way we expected them to.

When those situations occur, our parents have shown us by their own example ways to resolve them so that our relationships with each other aren't damaged. We'll talk more about how we resolve disputes with our siblings in the next chapter. In this section we want to share the ways we relate to our parents. For Duggar kids, that begins with how we talk to and with Mom and Dad.

Like most families, our parents desire that their relationship with us is one of love and mutual respect. Mom and Dad have also emphasized that they are there for us whenever we're going through a tough time and need someone to share our heart with. They've made it clear that we can always come to them and tell them *anything* and they'll be there to listen and, if need be, to give us counsel. They understand that sometimes girls just need to talk to someone but don't necessarily want a five-step solution to fix everything! Many times we just want someone to listen to what's going on in our lives.

We are reminded that the book of Proverbs is full of parents saying to their children, in various ways, "My son, my daughter, give me your heart. Hear my counsel. Listen to my instruction." In communicating with our parents about the challenges and struggles we are facing, we have found that they walked through similar experiences in their own youth, and they can share personal stories, encouragement, and advice on how to get through these difficult times.

I (Jinger) went through a couple of difficult stages when talking with Mom and Dad was both challenging—and healing. The first was when I was about five years old and we were living in a rented house near Little Rock while Dad was serving in the legislature there. One evening while Dad was driving the hour-long commute home from work, a tornado warning was issued for our area. Mom and Grandma nestled all of us kids into the bathtub, and we huddled there, praying and singing hymns as the tornado roared by a neighborhood not too far from ours.

For a long time after that I was fearful of death and of storms. There were many, many nights when I would wake up Mom and Dad in the middle of the night, worrying that another storm would come and kill us all. Or kill me. Or kill them and leave us kids to fend for ourselves.

When Dad asked if the girls would like to experience what it's like to go turkey hunting, Jinger took him up on the invitation.

Our parents have always encouraged us to come to them anytime, day or night, when we're frightened or having troubling thoughts. (Daddy says some nights they have a full and overflowing room full of Duggars!)

When I would go to my parents with my fears, they would snuggle me into their arms and reassure me. They would encourage me to look to God by quoting the words of David from the Psalms: "What time I am afraid, I will trust in Thee" (Psalms 56:3). Then they would pray with me and remind me of other Bible verses that promise God's love and care for us, such as God's promise "I will never leave thee, nor forsake thee" (Hebrews 13:5). Eventually I would go back to bed and sleep soundly.

Now when I meet a little girl who's afraid of storms, I tell her I used to be afraid, too, and I'd run to my parents' bedroom just as she's probably doing when the thunder rolls and the lightning crackles. And I tell her what my parents encouraged me to do every time I felt afraid: they would suggest that I focus on those reassuring Bible verses I'd memorized (such as Psalm 23) and that I shift my focus away from myself and my fears by praying for someone else who might be going through a scary or difficult time.

I grew out of my fear of storms just in time to hit another difficult bump in the road. It came when I was turning thirteen and entering the tough stage so many girls endure somewhere between twelve and sixteen. You're no longer a little girl, but you're not quite a woman. The hormones kick in. You suddenly notice boys. Confusing thoughts are zipping through your mind and sometimes lies fill your head, telling you things like "I'm ugly" or "I'm never gonna get a guy."

The lies in your head can seem random and constant, making you think you have to look a certain way or act a certain way. Self-acceptance becomes a major issue. You want to change your looks, your friends, your personality, everything. You want desperately to appear like a super-cool teenager, but at the same time, you may feel yourself inwardly spiraling downward into an endless well of self-doubt.

When I was in this stage, I went to my parents many a night, or I would confide in Mom during the day, sharing my worries or doubts about myself.

My parents responded with unwavering love and encouragement. Dad would say, "Jinger, as long as you keep talking, you will be okay!

You'll get through this. It's a season of your life, and things will get easier as you grow in your relationship with God."

Mom reminded me that when Jesus was tempted, He quoted Scripture. She wrote out verses for me to memorize from Romans 6 and other passages so that when the doubts or fears would sneak in, I could push them aside with assurances and truths from God's Word. As a family, we also memorized Ephesians 6:10–20 because it talks about the armor and weapons that we as Christians have to use against the attacks of Satan.

Mom also encouraged me to choose a "prayer target" and suggested that anytime I was tempted by negative thoughts or by worries and fears I could use that as a springboard to pray for someone I knew who needed God's salvation or just needed to draw closer to Him. She gave me a great mental exercise: every time the devil tries to tempt you to be fearful, to believe lies about yourself, or to get consumed with boy thoughts, take the focus off yourself by quoting God's Word and praying for someone else. Satan definitely doesn't want you praying, so eventually he'll back off!

Like Dad, Mom also assured me that this stage would soon pass. One day, when I was in the throes of self-doubt and tempted to let worrisome thoughts fill my mind, Mom asked me if it would be okay if she asked Jana to talk with me. I agreed. Jana opened up and shared about how during her teenage years she had experienced many of the same struggles, and as she applied these same principles to her life she was able to slowly get out of this same emotional rut. She said this emotional roller coaster affects a lot of teenage girls, but as you seek the Lord and grow in your relationship with Him you will be strengthened, and these trials will slowly fade away.

Mom knew that her and Dad's reassurance was helpful, but to hear it from an older sister who had been in the same stage not too long ago was even more powerful. Proverbs 19:20 tells us to "hear counsel, and receive instruction, that thou mayest be wise." I listened to Mom's and Jana's counsel, and the troubling thoughts soon lessened.

HEART-TO-HEART TALKS

MOM AND DAD DON'T just say, "You can talk to us anytime," and leave it at that. In addition to daily striving to keep up with our hearts, they also set aside time—usually on one Saturday a month—specifically for heart-to-heart family time. It's a dedicated time when each of us kids, one after another, spends time with them talking one-on-one, typically either in their bedroom or in the room we call our prayer closet. Sometimes we talk with Mom, sometimes with Dad, or sometimes with both together. Often to help get the conversation going, they'll ask us questions.

They've let us know that they are a "safe place" to share things and that we can tell them anything, no matter how hard it may be for them to hear.

So far, if they've been shocked by something we've said, they haven't shown it. And we know they will keep our issues private unless we agree that they can share them with a sibling, like Mom did when Jinger needed encouragement from Jana. As Dad says, they're not going to announce our worries or misdeeds as public prayer requests next Sunday at church!

Since our parents have a twenty-four-hour open-door policy, we sometimes come in at midnight, even 2 A.M., just to talk or share our heart. (If we come in too late, things *can* get a bit entertaining. Dad sometimes finds it hard to stay awake. It's not a matter of interest. But after all, it *is* 2 A.M., and even the Duggars are usually asleep by then. That's when Mom might give him a gentle nudge and say, "Jim Bob, wake up. We're still talking here!")

At the beginning of a heart-to-heart talk, Mom and Dad might start by asking, "How are you doing?"

Often we respond with a simple "Okay."

And of course, most parents can discern whether that means "good" or "not so good."

From time to time, they might ask other simple questions—about our favorite food, restaurant, candy, coffee, ice cream, board game, color, music, clothes, and more. These questions aren't just meant as icebreaker chitchat. Mom takes notes! She may have nineteen kids, but she wants to know every one of us in detail.

Inevitably, depending on the age of the child, the questions vary from "Have you been kind to your siblings when playing?" for younger kids, into "How's your thought life going?" for an older one.

Then, depending on which child they're talking with, they might pick a couple of different questions from this list to ask during talk time:

1. Who's your best friend? What qualities do you admire in him or her? Does this friendship tend to build you up or pull you down?

2. What do you want to do with your life? Whom do you want to be like? What skills do you want to develop? Do you wonder what God's will is for your life?

3. What books are you reading? What interests you in that book and how has it influenced you? Have you ever thought about writing a book? What topic would you write about? (*You might have guessed our answer to these last questions!*)

4. What things in our family discourage you? (Clutter? Conflicts with siblings? Lack of space? Rules? When others get into your stuff?)

5. What changes would you like to see in us (Mom and Dad)? (More time spent with the family? Greater spiritual leadership?)
6. What projects are you working on now? Who or what are you praying for? (Career training? Mentoring others?)
7. What things about yourself or your past would you like to change?
8. If you could ask God any question, what would you ask Him?
9. What things can I pray about for you?

These questions have changed over time, and of course the questions they ask depend on the age of the child having the heart-to-heart talk. Growing up with this kind of communication builds trust, and we feel the freedom to share our deepest thoughts, hopes, fears, and failures with our parents.

WHOSE RESPONSIBILITY IS IT?

WE KNOW THAT THIS family tradition of ours is pretty unusual. Maybe in your family, there's no way parents and kids can spend a whole day talking one-on-one. And actually, having a set day for family talk time may be the ideal, but it's *not* our parents' primary goal. Their priority is that we maintain open communication *at all times.*

Maybe you'd like to have this kind of open relationship with your parents, but you feel awkward suggesting it or just don't know how to make it happen. And even if your parents do set aside time for heart-to-heart talks with you, we know you may not find it easy to respond.

That's what happened when I (Jessa) was about thirteen. About that time, I started thinking, *If my parents really cared about me, they would be able to see that something is troubling me, and they'd help me work through it.*

But as much as I knew Mom and Dad loved me, and as hard as they tried to let me know they were there for me, they didn't ask the "ideal question" (whatever that was!) that would have opened the floodgates.

Ever been there? Thinking your parents just don't understand you? When that happens, it's easy for walls of bitterness and hurt to rise up as you sink deeper into your self-absorbed thinking and start believing your parents just aren't there for you when you need them most.

The truth is, they're probably much more "there" for you than you realize. But you may be stuck in a mind-set that makes you think it's *their* responsibility to figure out what's going on with you—when, most likely, you can't even figure it out yourself!

It finally dawned on me one day that the key was for me to take responsibility in initiating the conversation—and that it was *my* responsibility to respond honestly to their questions when they tried to have a heart-to-heart talk.

Instead of giving superficial answers to their questions, I attempted to be more thorough and open with my answers. But the change was hard. While I really wanted to

Our parents, Michelle and Jim Bob, value their relationship with Jesus as their top priority. Second to that comes their relationship with each other and with their family.

be honest, I also didn't want to "bother" them with everything, so I still held back some stuff.

That meant those issues built up and up and up until, and by the time I finally decided to open up to my parents, I felt almost like I was in a "crisis situation"! I would be so stressed that I couldn't get my thoughts into words, and then I would begin to worry:

What are my parents going to think about me if I share this with them?

What will others think if they find out?

Would I be better off not saying anything?

My parents reassured me that nothing I would ever say or do could change their love for me. Their love is unconditional. They also encouraged me to try to get everything off my heart. Mom compared it to getting a splinter in your foot. Unless you get all of it out, it will continue to cause you pain and can even become infected. Removing a splinter may be somewhat painful at first, but that is the only way to get long-term relief and bring healing.

I finally shared a small thing, just to see how they would react. Then a little more and a little more until it all came pouring out in a rush of sobs and jumbled-up phrases. After I shared, I felt so free inside, almost like a huge burden was lifted off my shoulders. This was one of the hardest things I had ever done, but it brought peace and strengthened my relationship with my parents. All of those fears that had held me back from talking had almost kept me from experiencing one of the most wonderful feelings in the world—a clear conscience.

All of us girls have realized that if we end up crying when we're talking to Mom and Dad (and Jill and Jinger are now the most likely to cry), it's usually because we've waited too long to share the concerns of our hearts.

After several heart-to-heart meltdowns, I (Jessa) have gotten better at opening up and talking about things that trouble me with Mom and Dad before the problems build up. That's not to say it's always easy, but the blessings and sense of freedom that come with being completely open and honest are wonderful. It means we feel understood by our parents, inside and out, and we know without a doubt that they accept us and love us unconditionally.

It's a sign of increasing maturity when a young person begins to develop these communication skills. Being open can spare us many troubles later on, as so many issues in adult life are a direct result of miscommunication or noncommunication.

IMPROVING YOUR RELATIONSHIP

HERE ARE SOME SUGGESTIONS for how you can improve your communication—and your relationship—with your parents.

If you visit our house, you might find yourself in the middle of a foursquare game the minute you walk in the front door!

Spend Time Together

SURE, YOU MAY LIVE in the same house, but how much time do you actually spend enjoying each other? If that sounds strange to you, we encourage you to give it a try. Even if you feel your relationship with your parents is strained, try just hanging out with them and watch for opportunities to start up a conversation.

In many homes, conversation flows easily around the kitchen table or across the kitchen counter as someone is cooking or preparing a meal. Ask your parents questions about their childhood and growing-up years. Share something funny that one of your friends or little siblings said. Find something to chat about, even if it's the weather. Small talk can help to keep your relationship healthy and create a foundation for discussing deeper issues.

Express Gratefulness

AS A FAMILY, WE resolve to weed out daily those attitudes of ungratefulness that sneak in and bring with them an air of discontent. For instance, around our house we are not allowed to say, "I'm bored." It is an expression of ungratefulness with a person's surroundings and a complaining attitude with the idea that one must be constantly doing something fun or entertaining in order to be happy.

Now, we must admit that there have been times when one of us dared to utter those taboo words, but Mom quickly cured us of our "boredom" with her nonchalant reply, "Well, if you can't think of anything to do, I certainly can!" and then she would put us to work! If we as sons and daughters take on a selfish "me-centered" attitude in life, we may begin to feel that our parents owe it to us to provide us with all the latest toys and gadgets, cute cars, and a fancy house. But the Bible says, "And having food and raiment, let us be therewith content" (1 Timothy 6:8). This means we should be content with the most basic necessities of life, and that anything beyond that is an extra bonus, not something we deserve or require.

Another thing that expresses ungratefulness is complaining about rules or family guidelines. It never does any good to throw a fit like a two-year-old! If there is something we really want to do but Mom and Dad don't agree, it's helpful to try to see things from their point of view. Our parents encourage us to talk to them and make a "wise appeal" (more about this later) if we feel something should be changed or done differently.

Parents work hard to provide for their family's needs and even some of the "wants." We need to constantly let them know we appreciate what they do, whether it's cooking supper, hosting a birthday party, paying for music lessons—or helping to put us through college! All of us, including parents, like to have our work and sacrifices acknowledged. We can really brighten a parent's day with a hug, a note of gratefulness, or a meaningful word of encouragement and appreciation.

Be a Blessing

DO YOUR PART. ACTUALLY *look* for ways to bless others. Help out around the house and watch for opportunities to do little jobs, like washing the dishes, taking out the trash, cleaning, organizing, or folding the laundry without being asked. Do your best to get along with your brothers and sisters so your home is a place of peace and joy where everyone feels safe and protected.

THE OBEDIENCE GAME

DUGGAR KIDS GROW UP playing the Obedience Game. It's sort of like Mother May I? except it has a few extra twists—and there's no need to double-check with "Mother" because she (or Dad) is the one giving the orders.

It's one way Mom and Dad help the little kids in the family burn off extra energy some nights before we all put on our pajamas and gather for Bible time (more about that in chapter 8). To play the Obedience Game, the little kids all gather in the living room. After listening carefully to Mom's or Dad's instructions, they respond with "Yes, ma'am, I'd be happy to!" then run and quickly accomplish the tasks.

For example, Mom might say, "Jennifer, go upstairs to the girls' room, touch the foot of your bed, then come back downstairs and give Mom a high-five." Jennifer answers with an energetic "Yes, ma'am, I'd be happy to!" and off she goes.

Dad might say, "Johannah, run around the kitchen table three times, then touch the front doorknob and come back." As Johannah stands up she says, "Yes, sir, I'd be happy to!"

"Jackson, go touch the front door, then touch the back door, then touch the side door, and then come back." Jackson, who loves to play army, stands at attention, then salutes and replies, "Yes, sir, I'd be happy to!" as he goes to complete his assignment at lightning speed.

Sometimes spotters are sent along with the game player to make sure the directions are followed exactly. And of course, the faster the orders can be followed, the more applause the contestant gets when he or she slides back into the living room, out of breath and pleased with himself or herself for having complied flawlessly. All the younger Duggar kids love to play this game; it's a way to make practicing obedience fun!

THE FOUR POINTS OF OBEDIENCE

THE GAME'S RULES (MADE up by our family) stem from our study of the four points of obedience, which Mom taught us when we were young.

As a matter of fact, as we are writing this book she is currently teaching these points to our youngest siblings. Obedience must be:

1. *Instant.* We answer with an immediate, prompt "Yes ma'am!" or "Yes sir!" as we set out to obey. (This response is important to let the authority know you heard what he or she asked you to do and that you are going to get it done as soon as possible.) Delayed obedience is really disobedience.

2. *Cheerful.* No grumbling or complaining. Instead, we respond with a cheerful "I'd be happy to!"

3. *Thorough.* We do our best, complete the task as explained, and leave nothing out. No lazy shortcuts!

4. *Unconditional.* No excuses. No, "That's not my job!" or "Can't someone else do it? or "But . . ."

THE HIDDEN GOAL WITH this fun, fast-paced game is that kids won't need to be told more than once to do something.

Mom would explain the deeper reason behind why she and Daddy desired for us to learn obedience. "Mom and Daddy won't always be with you, but God will," she says. "As we teach you to hear and obey our voice now, our prayer is that ultimately you will learn to hear and obey what God's tells you to do through His Word."

In many families it seems that many of the goals of child training have been lost. Parents often *expect* their children to know what they should say and do, and then they're shocked and react harshly when their sweet little two-year-old throws a tantrum in the middle of the grocery store. This parental attitude probably stems from the belief that we are all born basically good deep down inside, but the truth is, we are all born with a sin nature. Think about it: You don't have to teach a child to hit, scream, whine, disobey, or be selfish. It comes naturally. The Bible says that parents are to *"train* up a child in the way he should go: and when he is old, he will not depart from it" (Proverbs 22:6).

It's a parent's responsibility to train their children to behave with good character when they are young so that, by God's grace, as they continue to grow and mature, they will one day be loving, caring, and responsible adults. And while training in the middle of a misbehavior is always necessary, Mom has found that many of these situations can be avoided by training kids how to respond to a situation before it arises. Maybe you could call it *preventive parenting.*

For instance, during hot summer days growing up, Mom would occasionally let all of us have a Popsicle as a special treat. While we were picking out our favorite flavor, she would say, "After we're done with our Popsicles, what are we going to do with the wrapper and sticks? That's right. They go in the trash can—*not* in the yard."

Now, that's not to say we never dropped our Popsicle wrappers outside somewhere, but hearing that many times beforehand helped us remember—and saved Mom from having to correct us afterward.

It helps so much to have goals to aim for and learn the right responses to different situations. From the time we were young, as part of our homeschooling we would study a different character quality every month, memorizing its definition together as a family. A full list of all forty-nine character qualities, published by the Institute in Basic Life Principles, can be found on our website (www.duggarfamily.com), but we would like to list a few here:

- *Obedience* is the freedom to be creative under God-given authority.
- *Generosity* is realizing that all I have belongs to God and using it for His purposes.

- *Freedom* is not the right to do what I *want* but the power to do what I *ought*.
- *Self-control* is instant obedience to the initial prompting of God's Spirit.
- *Kindness* is seeing needs in the lives of others as opportunities to demonstrate my love for Christ.

Once we had recited the character quality definition of the week a few times, each one of us would write it out on a sheet of paper and decorate it with stickers and markers. Then we would post our decorative youthful artwork around the house. Mom always made learning fun!

As our family has memorized these and many other powerful definitions, we have gained a deeper understanding of what these words really mean.

A WISE APPEAL

NOW, WE ALL ACKNOWLEDGE that nobody's perfect, and that includes parents. Sometimes parents may ask you to do something or go somewhere when they're not fully aware of the details or how the request will affect you. When this happens in the Duggar family, our parents encourage us kids to make what we call a "wise appeal." It means we are expected to respectfully remind our parents of information they have forgotten or may not know, or things that are going on that might interfere with our carrying out their request. The key word here is *respectfully*. Sometimes this may include asking if it is okay to approach the project from a different angle—using a creative alternative, as long as it accomplishes the same ultimate goal (see Daniel 1).

When an authority asks us to do something, we should try to see from the authority's perspective, *how* and *why* he or she wants it done. If we feel we cannot follow through because the time frame is too short or we find it's unsafe or there are other obstacles hindering it from being accomplished, then it's time for a wise appeal.

Don't just *ignore* what the person in authority is asking. It is a poor representation of your character when you just avoid doing the requested job or activity altogether without attempting to make an appeal and explain why. Like Daniel in the Bible, who came up with an innovative alternative when he was asked to do something he knew was wrong, we must also formulate a creative alternative to present to the person in authority when needed. Don't argue in pride and try to convince the authority you have a better idea; instead, humbly make your case to the one in charge.

For example, if Mom asked Josiah to mow the lawn, he would ordinarily have no problem doing that. But maybe he already had plans to help Dad with a remodeling project at one of our rental properties. In that case, it's Josiah's responsibility to make a wise appeal by saying, "I would be glad to mow the lawn, but Dad and some of the others are in the middle of a tiling project and could use some extra help. Would it be okay if I did it later, or would you want to ask one of the other kids to do it?" More than likely she would agree that Dad could

use Josiah's help with the tiling, and she would have Joy or someone else mow the lawn.

A wise appeal starts by making sure our attitude is right. If we're in the middle of a really good book and don't want to leave it, that's not a good

Jessa and Jinger express their love for each other through this big hug!

enough reason not to help Mom when she asks us to do something. Appeals should not be made merely as an attempt to get out of doing work. On the other hand, if we've set up a time to mentor a younger friend and she is due to arrive in fifteen minutes, we might say, "Mom, I would be happy to help you, but Jamie's coming over at three for our mentoring time. Would it be okay if I did it later?"

Remember to always show respect to those in authority, even when you can't comply with what they want you to do. If you simply say, "Nope, I'm not gonna do that," you may end up getting in trouble because of your stubborn attitude as much as because you're refusing to do what's asked of you.

If you mouth off and say, "*Mom,* you know I can't go to the store now! Jamie's coming at three," your words and tone portray a condemning attitude that's far from respectful.

While some kids tend to take that approach and fire back a reason why they can't do something, others may say, "Sure, I'll do it," just to get their parent off their case. Maybe they really do plan to do it eventually, just not right now. Parents don't appreciate this, either, and you can be sure they will be disappointed later to hear "Oh, I forgot," or to hear you recite a long list of excuses why you didn't get it done. In the future this makes it hard for them to trust you and believe you will follow through

Mom and Jessa flash confident smiles before heading out on the skydiving airplane and parachuting from 12,800 feet.

with what you say you'll do. It is better to make a wise appeal if you honestly think you cannot do it right away.

Wise appeals are also necessary if, halfway through the task, you encounter some legitimate roadblock that hinders you from finishing the project. For instance, if the mower runs out of fuel, go back and report why you are unable to complete the mission. If you just think, *Well, that's that,* and quit, leaving the job half done, you can expect that when your parent comes to check up on the project, he or she won't be very pleased.

A wise appeal makes a parent, teacher, boss, or anyone else in authority happy because he or she appreciates your respectful attitude, even when you're asking to be excused from what you're being asked to do. This also applies if someone should ask us (we hope unintentionally) to do something dangerous or morally wrong. Even then, it's important to be humble, loving, respectful, and yet bold, as we state our reasons for not complying.

PARENTS STRUGGLE, TOO

WE'VE EXPLAINED THAT OUR parents encourage us to share our hearts with them, including our struggles. But it may surprise you to learn that they also open up their hearts to us in some ways. They don't go into unnecessary detail, but they aren't afraid to tell us their faults, and they want us to learn from their past mistakes and failures.

Dad has also asked us kids to please bring it to his attention if we see him raising his voice or talking with sharp words. Not that he has a major anger problem, but like everyone who lives and breathes, he's experienced anger at one time or another. Dad has told us that his own father was prone to angry outbursts. He has shared with us how hurtful and frightening his father's angry outbursts could be. As a result,

Dad committed early on to try to control his temper and spare his family from the anger that had caused him such discomfort as a boy.

That's not to say Dad never gets angry. But he doesn't express it in angry rants. When he's upset about something one of us kids has done (or about something thoughtless or mean that someone has done), he handles the situation directly—but calmly. If the culprit is one of the kids, he or Mom will take that one aside and speak to him or her quietly and respectfully. If a consequence is in order, it's handed down the same way—privately, calmly, and respectfully. Mom and Dad have made it a practice to praise in public, correct in private.

Years ago, Dad heard a man speak about his struggle with anger and how God had given him a creative way to handle it. Dad decided right then to implement the same strategy into his own life. That's when he told all of us kids if we ever sense that he's getting worked up about something, we have his permission to touch his arm gently and quietly say, "Daddy, I think you're getting angry."

It isn't that Dad doesn't *know* he's upset about something. Instead, the little hand on his arm reminds him how important it is for his family's well-being that he keep control of his temper. He told us to do that because he knows that words can come pouring out in anger that can't be taken back and can cause emotional scars even after apologies are given. These days, it seems like it rarely happens because Dad has really made it a point to keep his temper in check, and we all agree he has done a great job!

Some girls have confided in me (Jana) that they sometimes fear their dads because they have exploded into a rage, throwing things, slamming doors, even hitting or pushing their wives. They would probably shrug at examples of how our dad has expressed his anger in the past. But dad has felt bad about these situations and has quickly apologized. Over the years he has gotten much better about not letting things stir up a spirit of anger in him, but he would be the first to say he has not completely conquered it.

For example, one day not too long ago, Dad asked those of us who were working inside to clean the house before company arrived while he and a few of the other kids cleaned up outside. When he came in an hour or so later, the house was still a mess—and may have even looked worse than when Dad and the others went outside. The Duggars in charge of cleaning the living room and kitchen and emptying the downstairs trash cans had not done their jobs. Dad walked in the door, took one look at the house, and said loudly and sternly in an angry tone, "*Guys*, I asked you to clean this place up more than an hour ago, and look at it: it looks like a tornado has hit!"

Were those children (who shall remain nameless) wrong when they didn't do what Dad asked? Yes. Did they get in trouble for not carrying out their responsibilities? Yes.

But at the same time, Dad knew he had reacted with an attitude of anger, and that wasn't the behavior he wanted his children to imitate.

Later that evening he called all of us kids together to apologize. He said, "The situation wasn't as important as my wrong response. I reacted with anger, and I want to ask you all, Will you please forgive me?"

Did that make Dad look weak? Absolutely not! One lesson we Duggars are emphatically taught is that humility is not weakness. In fact, it can be just the opposite. It takes a strong man to recognize his own faults and apologize to his wife and children for them. Dad's humility—not only that day but every day—causes us to respect and admire him even more.

Dad's example to make things right has encouraged us to examine our own reactions to others and to take action when we need to admit we have done something wrong.

Mom, on the other hand, has a rather unique way of handling anger—even though she rarely gets angry. But when she does, she lowers her voice to a gentle whisper. That's right. No yelling. God convicted her of this early in her parenting as she realized the truth of Proverbs 15:1, which says, "A soft answer turneth away wrath, but grievous words stir up anger."

When Mom gets upset with one of us, she will take that child aside, get down to his or her eye level, and in a soft voice, almost whisper her words: "Josie, you may not dump your bowl of cereal on the table and smear it everywhere!" or "Jordyn, don't *ever* climb up on the outside of the staircase! That is very dangerous. You could fall off and hurt yourself!"

The long and short of it is, when Mom whispers, most likely someone's in trouble.

In contrast to Mom's quiet way of handling anger, I've seen the effects of out-of-control anger firsthand. The number-one painful thing girls talk about at the Journey to the Heart girls retreat—a ministry I am involved with—and almost always through tears and heartache, is anger in the home.

Mom is not only our mother but also our role model, teacher, and mentor. She's also someone we like to have fun with, including dressing up for a women's event that asked everyone to wear a fancy (and funny) hat.

Anger can cause lifelong damage to anyone, but especially to children. It can break apart families, destroy marriages, kill friendships, and even end careers. Dad has told us many stories of people who have gotten angry and lost control of themselves, as well as the consequences that followed. One employee at the grocery store where Dad used to work got mad at the boss for getting on to him, so he punched the boss with his fist! As you could guess, that was the end of his job.

Another young man my dad knew got angry with another driver in a road rage incident. They both ended up stopping at the side of the road and yelling at each other. One young man got so angry that he put his car in gear and rammed into the other guy. That day both young men's lives changed forever; one died, and the other ended up going to prison.

We know our parents aren't perfect—they are the first ones to admit this. But they have worked hard to teach us biblical principles and how they play out in our lives, and we are so thankful for the influence they are in our lives!

3

YOUR RELATIONSHIP WITH YOUR SIBLINGS

Becoming best friends

Behold how good and how pleasant it is
for brethren to dwell together in unity!
—Psalms 133:1

IT'S NOT ALWAYS EASY getting along with eighteen siblings. After all, with this many kids in the family we have just about every personality type possible. Some of us are easygoing, laid-back types, and others are constantly moving go-getters. Duggar kids range from outdoorsy types to computer geeks, animal lovers to bookworms. When one of us is sick or feeling discouraged about something, we can count on some siblings offering compassionate sympathy while others may share a pat on the back and say something like "Come on, you'll probably feel better if you get up. Let's go outside and play!"

With such a diverse assortment of personalities, interests, strengths, and weaknesses, siblings provide the perfect environment for relationship training. It might just be true that if you can learn to get along with your siblings, you can learn to get along with just about anybody!

Maybe if you have a sibling or two—or ten—you understand. And if you're an only child and don't have any siblings at all, maybe some of the stories we share in this chapter will give you ideas about how to relate more securely and pleasantly to other family members—and keep your friendships strong, too.

Duggar kids are just like human beings everywhere. We have faults and shortcomings that include the ability to irritate or mistreat others, especially our siblings. And also like most human beings, we have the natural tendency to overreact or to react inappropriately when someone, especially a sibling, misbehaves or treats us unfairly.

With a family as big as ours, the result could be a home that's a constant battleground of hot-tempered yelling, accusations, denials, hitting, name-calling, and general chaos. Instead, our parents work hard to make our house a peaceful, fun, comfortable, love-filled place where everyone is treated with patience and respect.

But that doesn't mean conflicts never occur.

Consider the time, about ten years ago, when there were "only" fourteen Duggar children, most of us still under the age of fifteen, and Dad bought some used lockers at an auction. We were so excited to have someplace to store all of our own personal treasures—like our private stockpiles of candy, for instance.

But then Jill opened her locker one day, looking forward to a sweet treat, and all she found was empty wrappers. Someone had stolen her candy!

"Who got into my locker?" she asked the rest of us.

Nobody offered up a confession.

"That's it. I'm checking teeth," she said. And so she began. With the determination of a no-nonsense dental detective (or perhaps a veterinarian checking the age of a horse), she insisted on looking inside each sibling's mouth. One by one, confused little ones opened their mouths while Jill peered in. And then she got to Joy.

"I can see blue in your teeth!" Jill announced matter-of-factly. "You ate my Jolly Ranchers!"

Case solved. At this point Mom and Dad got involved and they lovingly, but firmly, talked to Joy. "What did you do?" they asked.

Joy confessed she had opened Jill's locker looking for something and found the stash of candy and ate one piece, then a second, and kept going till she'd eaten all of it. She apologized (more about Duggar-style apologies later), and Jill quickly forgave her. Something every person needs to learn from an early age is that we can be forgiven for whatever we do wrong, but there are still consequences. So then the Duggar-family penalty was imposed: if you take something that isn't yours, you must repay it—and, oftentimes, double repay it to learn your lesson. When it was all said and done, Jill ended up with more candy than she'd had before, and Joy learned to never take something that doesn't belong to her.

Soon after that incident, we all got locks for our lockers!

OFFERING APOLOGIES AND FORGIVENESS

ONE OF THE WAYS our parents have taught us to keep our sibling relationships strong is to deal with offenses quickly. That means a prompt and meaningful apology.

Mom and Dad have taught us what a meaningful apology is *not*: It's not saying, "I'm sorry *but* . . ." And it's never saying things like "I'm sorry if you were offended," or "I'm sorry I got angry because you mistreated me." Mom and Dad make it very clear that we shouldn't point out others' mistakes or blame others for our wrong response.

When we make a true apology, we swallow our pride, apologize for what we did, and "own" our offense, regardless of what happened before or after it—even if we feel the other person was 90 percent wrong and we were only 10 percent wrong, we apologize for our 10 percent. Mom taught us from a young age to look the person in the eye and say, with a humble attitude, "Johannah, I was wrong for being selfish and taking the toy away from you. Will you please forgive me?"

But then comes the offended person's responsibility: forgiveness. Sometimes that seems harder than apologizing! Sometimes people think if they refuse to forgive someone, that's a way to get revenge. The truth is, bitterness will eat us up inside.

Dad says when you won't forgive, it's as if you're saying to the one who wronged you, "I'll show you! I'm going to make you suffer for how you hurt or offended me. You're going to be sorry now!" Then it's like you turn around and drink a cup of poison. Instead of getting revenge, you're really just hurting yourself.

Mom adds, "No one enjoys being around a bitter, angry, complaining, critical person!"

Years ago, Mom realized our family needed to memorize Matthew 18, the chapter in which Jesus teaches us how to deal with offenses and hurt feelings and resolve them. With as many people as we have in our household, we have a lot of opportunities to put this conflict-resolution stuff into practice!

Dad reminded us that when we pray the Lord's Prayer (Matthew 6:9–13) we are asking God

As the oldest girls, Jill, left, and Jana have been best friends all their lives. As our family grew, occasional challenges occurred among siblings, but Mom and Dad taught us to work through difficulties using biblical guidelines.

to forgive us to the same degree we forgive others. It says, "Forgive us . . . as we forgive." Dad asked us to think about those words and take them seriously. Even though we might not *feel* like forgiving someone, we must *choose* to forgive every person who offends us and do it even before they ask—and regardless of whether they ever *do* ask. We must come to the place where we say, "Lord, I choose to forgive (name of offender) for (name of offense)." It's a choice we can't afford *not* to make.

The choice to forgive doesn't always free that other person from the consequences of his or her wrong actions, but it frees the forgiver from negative feelings toward the offender. And if we still have feelings of bitterness, the Bible says it's important not only to forgive the other person, but also to go a step further and look for ways to bless him or her.

GOING THE SECOND MILE

DADDY SHARED WITH US the principle of "going the extra mile" from Matthew 5:41. In Jesus's day, the law required that any Jewish boy over the age of twelve could be forced away from his own concerns at any time to help a Roman soldier carry his pack for up to one mile in any direction. In much the same way, Simon of Cyrene was forced to bear the cross of Jesus (see Matthew 27:32).

The Jews of Jesus's day, of course, deeply resented this humiliating law and saw it as a symbol of foreign domination. You can imagine, then, their surprise when Jesus said, "go with him *two* miles."

Jesus knew that by going the second mile, the offended one would be set free to show God's love to the offender. Picture the Roman soldier saying, "Okay, you're relieved from your duty now; you've gone your mile," and hearing the other person respond, "I'd like to carry your pack for you another mile."

What do you think the first question out of that soldier's lips would be? No doubt, you guessed it. He would say, "Why are you doing this?"

And that person would have an open door to say, "Well, because there was this Man named Jesus who taught me to go the second mile."

Don't you know that message would fall on open ears! That soldier would want to know what could motivate someone to show such undeserved kindness.

LEARNING A MEMORABLE LESSON

JESSA AND I (JANA) got a memorable lesson in how that works when Jessa was six and I was eight. At the time, we lived in a four-bedroom house, and Jill and Jinger shared one room, and Jessa and I shared another.

It's hard to imagine it now, but at the time Jessa and I really didn't get along—which is probably why our parents put us in the same room, so we could work on our relationship. We shared a bunk bed; I was on top, and Jessa was on the bottom.

Every night, as I was trying to go to sleep, Jessa would kick my mattress: *Thump. Thump. Thump.* I would ask her to stop, but she would keep right on kicking. This continued until I called Mom in and Jessa got in trouble. But only a few nights later, she'd be at it again: *Thump. Thump. Thump.* "That bother you up there, Jana?" she would say with a giggle.

(Note: This was early in the development of Mom and Dad's parenting skills, and they had not yet adopted some of the rules and practices we'll describe a little later.)

Our parents were tirelessly consistent about getting on to Jessa. But Jessa, likewise, was tirelessly consistent with her aggravating ways. Repeatedly, Mom and Dad corrected Jessa. And each time, they would have her come back in and apologize to me. Then we would give each other a hug, but still, the two of us just couldn't get along. Finally,

I began to simply avoid Jessa whenever I could because it seemed she was always looking for ways to annoy me.

One night during our family devotions, which we call Bible time, we read about the apostle Peter. I remember thinking he must have had an annoying person like Jessa in his life because he asked Jesus, "How many times can my brother offend me, and I still forgive him? Seven times?"

Jesus said, "Not seven times, but seventy times seven." Now, He wasn't saying that forgiving 490 times was the limit. (Because if that was the case, I thought, I could've probably stopped forgiving Jessa right then!) Dad explained that Jesus meant "You keep forgiving your brother as long as I keep forgiving you."

Even at that young age, I knew Jesus had already forgiven me for way more mistakes than Jessa had even thought of making.

I asked Mom what she thought I should do, and she told me, "Jana, if you really want your sister to be nice to you, make it a point to be nice to her, even when she's mean to you." Then she shared with me what Jesus said in Matthew 5:44: "Love your enemies, bless them that curse you, do good to them that hate you, and pray for them which despitefully use you, and persecute you."

Mom said an enemy could be understood as "anyone who invades your territory," and Jessa sure was intruding—on my bunk bed, my sleep, and my disposition! Mom encouraged me to think of something nice I could do for her. So even though I didn't want to and definitely didn't feel like doing it, after praying about it I decided to give Jessa something that was very special to me.

Jill and I, as the oldest of the girls, had each been given matching pink jewelry boxes, and we both *loved* those beautiful boxes. It was hard to think of giving away one of my most treasured possessions— especially to someone I wasn't happy with. But I tucked a few other childish but special-to-me things inside my jewelry box and then wrapped it up along with some candy. A little later, I told Jessa I had something to give her. I told her I loved her and handed her my gift.

From my perspective, I (Jessa) admit to having been a very strong-willed child. I enjoyed irritating my big sister Jana because I thought it was funny to see her response. I knew how to get under her skin! Now I know that what I really wanted, deep down, was for her to pay attention to me, and by aggravating her, I definitely got her attention.

The heart change for me began that day when she handed me that unexpected gift. I couldn't believe it at first. What kid doesn't like getting a gift? I was thinking I was getting a head start on birthday gifts, but I was pretty sure my birthday wasn't anytime soon. Then Jana told me she loved me and just wanted to give me a gift to *show* me she loved me.

When I tore off the paper and saw her beautiful jewelry box, I was speechless. Even though I was only six, I understood what a treasure she was giving me. I knew how much she loved that jewelry box!

After that, somehow, it was no longer fun to annoy Jana. That's not to say I instantly stopped all the annoying habits I'd developed in my young life so far, but never again did I view Jana as someone who was

Our family travels together often—and of course we have our conflicts. Here we are at the Kennedy Space Center in Florida. Notice our matching outfits!

fun to harass. From that time on, we began to spend more time play-ing together and doing things alongside each other, and she continued to show me how much she loved me in different ways.

Today, we're close friends as well as sisters, but I know this might not be the case if Jana hadn't forgiven me and taken that selfless step, way back in our childhood, to invest in my life and show me that she loved me. She truly demonstrated to me the principle behind the verse that says, "Where your treasure is, there will your heart be also" (Mat-thew 6:21).

Today we know families where adult siblings still can't get along because all throughout their growing-up years their relationships fo-cused more on irritating each other than on being friends. We're so thankful our parents have put such a priority on helping us overcome those challenges at a young age. And we encourage all of you older girls who are reading this book to see that if you have a younger sibling who seems to make a hobby of constantly getting on your nerves, it's most likely a desire for your acceptance. As you include your little sis-ter or brother in your life and show genuine love, even when it's con-trary to what might seem like a natural reaction, we predict you'll see a turnaround in your relationship.

If your problem is with a sibling, friend, or even an enemy, the basic principles are still the same. God commands us to forgive those who have wronged us or offended us. And then He wants us to go a step further, that "second mile," and actually bless our offenders with kindness and prayer. Years ago, Mom and Dad gave us kids a wonderful example of blessing an enemy; it's one that we remember to this day.

BLESSING YOUR "ENEMY"

OUR PARENTS HAVE BEEN in the real estate business for more than thirty years, and one of the ways they support our family is through the income from rental properties. Years ago, we were building the house we now live in, and money was very tight. Our family really needed the income from every property we had rented.

But one tenant in a commercial building stopped paying. Every month he would promise Dad he'd pay up soon. Next week for sure, he would say. But next week turned into next month, and no payment was made. Months went by, and no rent was paid. Finally, as much as he disliked doing it, Dad had to evict the tenant. But the guy wouldn't leave! The local sheriff had to get involved, and it was a very unpleasant experience for everyone. But after they finally got him out, the unpleasant incident worsened when Mom and Dad saw the inside of the building: it had been vandalized. Walls had been spray-painted, electrical switches had been smashed with a hammer, and we found out the tenant had also drilled holes in the roof just out of meanness. To return it to rentable status required a lot of extra time and money we could not afford.

Meanwhile, we learned that the tenant had done the same thing to previous landlords, changing his personal and business name to avoid detection.

Shortly after he moved out of our building, we were surprised to learn that another property owner in our area had leased a commercial building to the man—even after Dad warned him about the man's prior offenses.

The unscrupulous tenant had cost our family a lot, and it would have been easy to feel resentful toward him. But instead Mom sat us all down, and together we prayed for the man's soul. She asked the Lord to bring people into his life who would point him to a relationship with God and that God would bless him with the character qualities he lacked, including honesty and integrity. Mom also asked God to heal him of the alcoholism that held him in a tight grip and also that he'd no longer be controlled by anger.

Then Mom asked us kids to think about what we could do to bless him.

It's normal to think of seeking revenge against someone who's wronged us. But again and again, God's Word teaches us that forgiveness heals in ways far beyond our understanding. And that was the powerful lesson Mom was demonstrating for us that day.

We made some homemade bread and honey butter, loaded up the van, and drove down the road to the man's new offices. Mom and I (Jill) and a couple of the other kids took the gift to him.

You can imagine the shock on his face when Mom said, "Hello. I'm Michelle Duggar, Jim Bob's wife, and we've brought you a little gift."

When we handed him the bread and honey butter, he quietly said, "That's very Christian of you." We wished him well, and returned to the van. He never apologized for his misdeeds, and we have no way of knowing what impact our unexpected gift had on him. But that wasn't the point. That day Mom was teaching us kids what Jesus meant when He told us to bless our enemies. Not that this man was an enemy in the normal sense of the word. But he had wronged us, and the experience could have left a brand of bitterness on our family for years to come. Instead, we saw just the opposite demeanor—humility and grace—in the character of our parents as they emphasized to us that people are far more important than things.

PRACTICING CONFLICT RESOLUTION

BECAUSE LOVE AND CHRIST-LIKE character have always been their desire for us kids, Mom and Dad are constantly teaching us, by their words as well as their actions, how to resolve our differences in ways that keep our relationships with each other strong and healthy. They have encouraged us to not hold a grudge or give someone the silent treatment—ignoring each other and with our body language saying, *I'm mad at you, and I don't want to be around you.* Instead, our parents encourage us to take care of an offense quickly and to do it before the day is over (see Ephesians 4:26). And then, once it's resolved, it's over. No hard feelings. We give each other a hug and go back to being best friends.

Apologies and forgiveness are crucial to this process, but we are learning that many of these ill feelings can be avoided from the start if we have a correct response at the onset of a situation. Proverbs 15:1 says, "A soft answer turneth away wrath; but grievous words stir up anger." This is why Mom works hard to respond to frustrating situations with a soft, almost-whisper voice—and encourages us to do the same. She's seen that responding with loud, angry words only serves to bring more heat to the confrontation.

Mom had her hands full with infant twins John-David and Jana plus toddler Josh. Little did she know then that God would give her and Daddy sixteen more children in the years ahead.

Words are like toothpaste in the sense that once they come out of our mouths, they are not going back in. When we find ourselves in the middle of a conflict where an argument is erupting or a wrong is being committed against us, Mom encourages us to think before we speak and ask God to help us have a soft answer.

TALKING SWEET

IT IS UNDERSTOOD IN our household that tattling—taking a grievance straight to Mom and Dad—is not the proper way to handle a dispute. If we complain to Mom and Dad, we know that their first question will be "Did you talk sweet?" If our answer is no, we have no business coming to Mom and Dad.

In Matthew 18, Jesus tells us that if our brother (or anyone) has offended us, we are supposed to go to that person and try to work things out in a kind and gentle way. Only after we have tried to encourage offenders to "turn their heart toward God and do what is right" (as Mom explains it) should we then bring the problem to the one in charge. Mom would remind us that our motive should not be to expose sin or evil deed, but to *restore* the "offender" to a right relationship with God and the people they've offended.

So here's how it works: Let's say Jill and I (Jana) are youngsters again, and Jill takes my cupcake. I can't first run to Mom and Dad and yell, "Jill took my cupcake!" That would be tattling. To be a restorer, I need to sweetly ask Jill to give it back to me. My natural tendency is to say, "Jill, you give that back, or you're in big trouble!" but that's not how to restore the relationship. Instead, I need to say, "Jill, would you please do what is right and give my cupcake back?"

If Jill doesn't return the cupcake (preferably uneaten), *then* I go to Mom or Dad with the problem. And most likely, Jill will face some consequences that give her a clear picture of what she did wrong. Mom and Dad guide the younger Duggar kids through this conflict-resolution training several times a day. This is not something that comes natural. It is learned behavior. Our parents have tried to be consistent, and they have seen it pay off.

Our parents have told us that a true friend is someone who encourages us to do what is right. As brothers and sisters, we're also friends. We each have a responsibility in the Duggar family to keep one another accountable. So if I (Jinger) see James ride down the driveway on Justin's new bicycle without permission and then leave it lying in the mud behind one of the cars, I don't tell Mom about it. I first go to James and encourage him to do the right thing: move the bike, clean off the mud, and then apologize to Justin for mistreating his new bicycle and for riding it without first asking Justin for permission.

If James refuses or says he'll do it later, then I've done all I can, and now it's time to get a parent involved. I would ask James to come with me to talk it over with Mom and Dad—and again, the conversation needs to unfold in a sweet, respectful tone. Our heart's motive here is so important. It should be our goal to see relationships restored, not merely to be the first one to expose others' misdeeds to Mom or Dad. Mom will often ask us, "Are you looking to be a restorer or an exposer?"

It takes a little while for the youngest ones to understand this system and get the hang of it. But those of us who are older can clearly understand how it helps maintain the peace in our family's home. As we have resolved to respectfully work out sibling arguments on our own, we find that most issues can be resolved without having to take it to a parent. Practicing this from an early age has proven to be beneficial preparation for adult life and going into the workplace, because the core principles for conflict resolution are the same—no matter our age.

SAYING "PLEASE DON'T"

ANOTHER SIMPLE DUGGAR FAMILY tradition that's crucial when one person is annoying another are the words "Please don't." In our family, those two code words mean "Don't do that again."

For example, if Jeremiah grabs his twin brother Jedidiah around the neck and wants to wrestle, Jed has two choices. He can take him on and have a friendly wrestling match, or he can say, "Please don't," and the wrestling stops. Jeremiah *must* stop wrestling with Jedidiah. That's the rule. No yelling, "Quit it!" or, "Stop it!" or, "I'm gonna tell on you." When a Duggar says, "Please don't," that's to be the end of it, and if the person doing the pestering doesn't stop, he or she is in trouble.

Mom and Dad also teach us that we need to be aware of what we're doing with our siblings and stop our own annoying behavior before it gets to the "Please don't" stage. For example, if Jackson is whistling in Jason's ear while he's trying to concentrate on reading a book, and it's clear Jason doesn't like it, Jackson should ask himself, *Am I the only one enjoying this?*

If one person is having fun and the other isn't, then, as Dad says it, "There is something wrong with this picture!" It's called *aggravating*, or around our house, "stirring up strife." And the aggravating behavior needs to stop; the one-sided fun is over.

SHARING PRACTICAL JOKES

NOW, AROUND OUR HOUSE there is a lot of fun and laughter throughout the day. Someone tells a funny joke or story, or plays a practical joke on someone, or someone does something that isn't meant to be funny but turns out that way. We love having fun together as long as it doesn't get out of hand.

A few years ago the Bates family, who also have nineteen children, came to Arkansas for a visit and to help us with some tree work after a big ice storm had hit our area. One afternoon, Dad was running some errands with Grandma Duggar when they decided to stop for some ice cream. As they pulled in to the parking lot of the ice cream shop, they noticed the Bates van parked by the right side entrance, and they saw Mrs. Kelly and several of her kids in the store. Dad pulled up and parked beside the Bates van, and as he and Grandma were getting out, he saw the oldest daughter, Michaela, sitting in the van with some of the littlest Bates kids.

Grandma and Dad opened the van door to say hi to Michaela, and then Dad got an idea. "Hey, why don't I pull your van around to the other side of the building to play a joke on your mom?" They all laughed at the thought of the rest of the family coming out with hands full of ice-cream cones and just assuming they'd forgot which side of the shop they'd parked on. Dad hopped in as the driver, and Grandma rode shotgun as they zipped around the back to the other side of the building.

But at that exact moment, one of the Bates girls in the ice-cream shop (not to mention any names, but hers is spelled E-R-I-N) looked up and started screaming to her mom that she just saw some guy drive off in their van. Then they both started screaming for the person scooping the ice cream, "Call the police! Call the police! Someone just hijacked our van!"

The guy whipped out his cell phone and hurriedly dialed 9-1-1. About that time they saw the van reappear on the other side of the building with Grandma Duggar in the passenger seat wearing a big

We love visiting the Bates family at their home in Tennessee, shown here, or having their family visit us. But because both families have nineteen kids (and counting!), it's a houseful.

grin on her face. They were still in shock, but they told the guy on the phone with the police, "Oh, it's just Grandma!"

Then they all came running out and told us how badly they had been frightened. But once their nerves had calmed down, everyone had a good laugh. Then they warned Dad, "Beware. What goes around, comes around!" And they assured him they would be looking for an opportunity to pull a little prank on him as well.

A few days later as Dad was burning a big pile of tree limbs that had fallen in the ice storm, he left one of the boys to keep an eye on the fire for a while. Mr. Bates got the idea to have one of the kids come running into the house yelling, "Fire! Fire!" and then everyone else was to cause a commotion like it was something serious. Well, it worked beautifully. We had never seen Dad move so fast! He jumped up out of his chair and quickly began filling up a big trash can full of water. Then he took off for the front door, hollering for help.

When he got outside, Mr. Bates announced this was Dad's payback and it was all a planned joke. There *was* a fire, but it was just the same controlled burn Dad had left an hour before. We all had a good laugh, and Dad may have learned his lesson when it comes to playing practical jokes on the Bateses!

LAUGHING WITH, NOT AT

USUALLY STORIES LIKE THESE are hilariously recounted when we all get together in the evenings for family devotions, or as we call it, Bible time. Almost every night around eight thirty our family gathers, usually in the boys' room, to discuss the happenings of the day and the plans or events on the Duggar schedule for the following day. Then we pray together and read a passage of Scripture (sometimes the Proverb that corresponds to the day of the month) and discuss how it applies to everyday life. Each one of us has an opportunity to share.

One night during Bible time, Josiah told how he and John were cruising down the road at fifty miles per hour in Dad's one-ton Dodge pickup, which is equipped with a tow truck wheel-lift on the back. Someone had forgotten to shut off the lift's power switch, and Josiah accidentally bumped the remote control with his foot, causing the arm to lower down to the road. Like a hydraulic jack, it lifted the rear tires of the truck up off the payment, and suddenly the back end of the truck skidded around into the ditch on the opposite side of the two-lane road.

It had to be a terrifying few seconds as the truck seemed to be picked up and spun around from the back by a huge, invisible hand and the guys suddenly found themselves staring out the front windshield up into the sky, bewildered by what had just happened! Thankfully no one was injured and by the time they drove the truck back home, Josiah was ready to share at Bible time, "You're not gonna believe what happened!"

We were grateful the incident had a good outcome. When Josiah shared his story, no one criticized or put him down for what had happened. Putting someone down, being critical, or making fun of someone by mocking or even calling names is not showing respect. Whether it's done in jest or with a spirit of cruelty, it can cause hurt that lasts a lifetime. Realizing how close they came to such a dangerous situation, we all took a moment to pray together and thank God for His providential protection, even for the fact that there was not a car coming in the other direction.

EARNING RESPECT

WHEN YOU GROW UP seeing how Scripture speaks to every area of life and how biblical principles make it possible to maintain close and loving relationships between yourself and your siblings, you see how the same practices carry over into relationships with others outside the family.

It's so easy to get upset when someone does something irritating or unfair or even damaging. But when we respond with love and respect for the other person, and with an attitude of humility rather than self-righteousness, the relationship can be strengthened rather than weakened.

Mom and Dad tell us that friends may come and go throughout our lives, but our brothers and sisters will *always* be our siblings, so it is especially important to keep these relationships strong and full of love and respect.

Sometimes it's easy to become frustrated when younger siblings pretend to temporarily have hearing problems when we're trying to talk to them, or when they leave toys scattered around our bedroom floor for the umpteenth time. In these situations, Mom and Dad have reminded us that respect is something to be earned, not demanded.

To maintain order and harmony in the home, we have always had a "chain of command," with Mom and Dad at the top and the "command" passing down the birth-order line from eldest to youngest. This is *not* something that lets older siblings assign their responsibilities to someone else. And it doesn't mean the older siblings have little servants waiting on them hand and foot. That's never allowed! The system is for those times when an older child encourages a younger child to do what is right or not do something wrong, and the younger child is expected to listen.

If I (Jinger) am babysitting my younger siblings and I say, "All right, kids, playtime is over. Let's clean up the house before bedtime," then all the kids know they're expected to stop what they're doing and start straightening up the house.

Mom and Dad have banned the phrases "You can't tell me what to do!" and "You're not my boss!" from our home, and they remind the younger children that their older siblings are their elders and they should treat them as such. So Johannah can ask Josie to help her pick up the toys in the playroom, and Josie needs to do it. Josiah can ask James not to whistle in the car, and he needs to stop. Joy can call all her younger siblings out to the bus after a road trip and delegate tasks to get the bus back in order, and everyone needs to listen to her instructions and cooperate.

This process has been very beneficial and has helped our family work together as a team. As long as the older siblings are telling the younger ones to do something good and right, something Mom and Dad would agree with, the younger ones need to listen and comply. And if they can't comply for some reason, they are encouraged to graciously explain why but with a respectful attitude, and not by smarting off with "I'm not gonna do it, and you can't make me!"

As older siblings, we have found that one of the fastest ways to earn respect from younger siblings is by respecting them. Sure, they may be half our age, but they are people, too, and they appreciate being treated with respect, just as we do.

When one of us complains about a younger sibling ignoring us or not being willing to listen to our advice, Mom says, "I know you want them to listen to you and respect you, but have you taken time to listen to them and hear what they have to say?"

Her words make us stop and realize how often we may have been too busy to hear them tell their favorite joke (yes, the same one we have heard over and over at least twenty times). Or to hear them excitedly tell us about the new words they are learning to read. Or maybe to listen to them play a violin piece they've been working hard on for several weeks.

When I (Jessa) was young, the thing that meant the most to me was seeing my older siblings enjoy my sense of humor. I know now that I didn't always have the funniest wisecracks or jokes to share, but I really felt loved and important when they listened to me and laughed at things I thought were funny.

Jinger has a special talent when it comes to musical abilities. She has always been diligent in her music practice and has really excelled. She is concert-pianist material! But when she was younger, there was a time when she compared herself to some of us other siblings, and I could tell she was a bit discouraged. Different ones of us were able to cheer her on with an encouraging word here and there, and today, she's the one giving us piano-playing tips!

As older siblings, our words and actions have so much power—they can either boost or shoot down our younger brothers' and sisters' self-esteem. Mom and Dad have encouraged us to praise the good character we see in our siblings instead of always focusing on the negative things. Instead of focusing on the food still stuck to the corner of the table after a little one tried to wipe it down, we've learned to praise their efforts in doing the job in the first place.

Mom explained that *praise* is not the same thing as *flattery*. Praise focuses on character qualities such as diligence, attentiveness, or cre-

Our film crew posed us in front of an old, abandoned
house in our area for a recent photo shoot.

ativity, while *flattery* is saying things like "You're so gorgeous" or "You're so smart" or "You're the best violinist in the whole world." Flattery can create a wrong attitude of pride because it focuses on outward appearance or God-given talents—things that individuals can't rightfully take the credit for.

Don't get us wrong; we should definitely be telling our little sister that we like her hairstyle or that her outfit is adorable. She needs to hear that from us more than from anyone else. But it is only half as important as her hearing us say we were blessed by her initiative in cleaning up the kitchen without being asked, or her generosity in sharing her candy with her little brother.

We've heard it said, "Be careful what you praise someone for, because he or she will want to do more of it." And we've found this to be true. As we have praised a sibling for good character, we see him or her work even harder at the task in the future. Younger (and older) siblings grow and thrive on praise and acceptance.

When you're trying to gain respect, it never *ever* helps to say things like "I wish you would just go away!" or "You're always getting on my nerves!" Something else that is known to cut deep is name-calling of any sort, even jokingly. If our siblings hear anything from us, it should be things like "You're so much fun to be around" or "You've got a great sense of humor." And if, for some reason, we can't think of anything else to say, we can always tell them, "I love you so much!"

As older siblings, we have had many times when younger siblings want to be just like us, whether it's dressing like us or wanting to go where we go or even wearing the same hairstyle. An incident many years ago served as a lesson to us all. A younger sibling asked, "What kind of ice cream are you getting?" and the frustrated older sibling replied, "You don't have to always copy everything I do! Why don't you just pick out your own flavor?"

Mom immediately took that older sibling aside and shared how much hurt and devastation a remark like that causes. She explained that the greatest form of admiration is imitation, and instead of being upset when a younger sibling wants to imitate us, we should realize that the young one is looking up to us and thinking the world of us. They want to be just like us, and one jabbing remark like that could greatly damage the relationship.

Apologies were made, and the younger sibling readily forgave. The older sibling resolved to never speak demeaning words like that again but rather to embrace and uplift this sibling, and today, these two continue to be the best of friends.

One thing that is sure to build respect is to ask a family member to point out our "blind spots." From time to time, and usually during every heart-to-heart talk, Mom and Dad have asked us kids to do this for them—to lovingly and respectfully point out things they may have unknowingly done to offend us or things they may have done that embarrassed or irritated us. They are willing to calmly listen to what we have to say and then apologize for misunderstandings or other things that have hurt us. That practice has given us older kids the courage to do the same with our younger siblings.

You can be sure this is *not* easy! It's especially hard not to react or want to defend ourselves. We call them "blind spots" for a reason—because often, we have a hard time seeing these actions and behaviors. They are like those spots from inside a vehicle as we're driving down the road and about to change lanes. We look out the rear- and side-view mirrors and don't see anything. But if we rely only on the mirrors and don't physically turn our head and look around before merging lanes, we're likely to hit the car that was there all along but was "hidden" in our blind spot.

I (Jessa) had an experience like that several years ago when I was a new driver. I went to the local grocery store to pick up some food for supper, and as I was backing out of my parking space, there was a car behind me that I couldn't see in any of my mirrors. But it was there nonetheless, and I ran right into it. I quickly pulled back into my parking space and got out to inspect the damage. My vehicle was fine, but I had put a large dent between the rear wheel well and the back fender of the other car. I had to wait for the lady to come out of the store, and then make restitution for the damage I had caused. I certainly didn't ram into her car on purpose. But just the same, the damage was done, and I was responsible.

In the same way, we sometimes do things that unknowingly hurt our siblings They may not come out and say, "You hurt me when you said or did such-and-such," but when we ask them to share these things and they know we won't react harshly or defensively, trust is built in our relationship.

BEING A LOYAL SIBLING

WE WANT TO TOUCH briefly here on the topic of loyalty among siblings and being willing to stand up for and encourage one another even when others make fun or tease. This is something that is stressed in the Duggar household. If someone is teasing our little brother because he's short for his age, or if a friend is about to pull a prank that would bring embarrassment on an unsuspecting sibling, we want to gently and lovingly take a stand and say, "Hey, that's not very nice. Let's not do that," or "I'd appreciate it if you wouldn't talk that way about my sister."

Likewise, if someone is making a joke of a sibling's outfit choice or hairstyle, we siblings should never join in or laugh along with the "joker." Disloyalty among siblings, even in the smallest incidents, can cause hurt feelings that can last a lifetime. To rephrase an old saying: Sticks and stones may break a person's physical bones, but mocking or scorning words will most definitely break a person's spirit and destroy his or her self-confidence.

As an example, in Arkansas, teens can get their learner's driver's license at the age of fourteen, and in the Duggar family, the first vehicle we usually learn to handle is the fifteen-passenger van. As a prerequisite, years before this, Dad starts us off on the riding lawn mower, so by the time we get our permit, we are comfortable behind the wheel. However, in the first few months, new drivers in our family assume the responsibility of driving our family to and from church on Sunday mornings, and it can be a little intimidating to have thirteen backseat drivers all trying to tell you to "Slow down!" or "Speed up!" and "Don't forget to turn your blinker on."

Mom and Dad have stressed that there's a distinct line between giving advice and degrading someone as a person. We have had friends overreact with some of our siblings and insinuate that they don't want

Duggar kids learn to drive first by being assigned lawn-mowing duties on the riding mower. Then they move up to driving the RTV around the property. Joy, shown here chauffeuring some younger Duggars, now has her learner's permit and is an excellent driver.

to be a passenger in the vehicle the sibling is operating—or even come right out and tell the sibling that he or she is a bad driver. That's definitely a situation when we will speak up and say, "Aww, that's not nice to say. He's actually a very good driver! Probably better than I was at his age."

Our parents have set an example for us in giving lots of encouragement and positive reinforcement to new drivers by saying, "Good job on making that turn" and "You're getting a lot smoother with your acceleration and braking." Our parents have encouraged us not only to stand up to others when they are putting down or mocking our siblings but also to go a step further and seek to constantly communicate the love and respect we hold toward one another.

For instance, Josiah recently started driving our family's bus, and even though he's just sixteen, he handles it very well. Even if we're a little nervous when a new driver is at the wheel, we resolve to give advice only when necessary and to praise the new driver to our friends, pointing out that he or she is a cautious and safe driver.

We have found that when friends hear us speak words of affirmation and praise about our siblings, the chances that they will speak negatively or poke fun at them are much smaller. We've found that it's refreshing when people sincerely build each other up instead of look for something to criticize and or critique. By God's grace, this is something all of us are trying to focus on in our lives.

BEING A SERVANT-LEADER

BECAUSE ALL OF US siblings are close and because we enjoy being together, we're always overjoyed to learn that another Duggar brother or sister is on the way. Since we were very young, Mom was always good to let us help out with the baby in ways that were age-appropriate. Mom would usually let us pick out an outfit for the littlest Duggar or let us rock the baby to sleep during naptime. And as the baby began eating his or her first table foods, we were able to help with feeding Cheerios or little jars of baby food. Looking back, we jokingly say it was like having live baby dolls. Of course, Mom was right there helping us all the time, but we absolutely loved getting to help out, and it was never considered drudgery.

As our family grew, we established the "buddy system," which pairs all of us older guys and girls with a younger "buddy." The buddy system has proved helpful time and again—especially with keeping track of everyone when we're making our way through an airport or sightseeing in a busy place like New York City. We all look out for each other so no one gets lost or separated from the group.

Of course, Mom and Dad are still Mom and Dad, and they're constantly filling that role with each one of us as our number-one buddies. But we older kids enjoy being able to help out whenever we can. We typically assist the littlest ones in ways such as fixing their hair or filling their plate at mealtime, or helping out with their music practice. Occasionally we may substitute for Mom in teaching a phonics lesson.

But lest you get the wrong impression, be assured this is not a one-sided ordeal. We also encourage our little buddies to practice doing things on their own and to help us with chores, working alongside us as we scrub dishes or work in the garden. This helps them grow and mature with the understanding that the world doesn't revolve around them. As Mom has told us repeatedly, "A person will be blessed with true happiness and joy only when their focus in life is on what they can give, not get." The Duggar household runs the smoothest when everyone—young and old—to the best of their ability, makes it their goal to serve and give 110 percent.

In Matthew 23:11–12, Jesus said, "He that is greatest among you shall be your servant. And whosoever shall exalt himself shall be abased; and he that shall humble himself shall be exalted." By looking for ways to serve our younger siblings, we older kids have the opportunity to display servant-leadership, something Jesus calls every Christian to do. This attitude helps the younger kids respect us, and in turn, they desire to be a servant-leader toward their younger siblings. This mind-set has strengthened and brought us closer as a family, and it has helped us learn to work together as a team.

SHARING LOSS

WE WERE THRILLED WHEN Mom became pregnant in 2009 with the baby who turned out to be our sweet Josie. And when Josie was born in December of that year, nearly fifteen weeks early, she weighed one pound, six ounces. Her head was the size of a cue ball, and her body was oh so tiny.

Mom had suffered a nearly fatal episode of preeclampsia, and we all wanted nothing more during that time than to be together, cling to each other, and pray together as we thanked God for His mercy in sparing both Mom and Josie. No one thought it odd when Dad said the whole family would be moving to Little Rock for a few months so we could be together until Josie was ready to come home. That's what we wanted.

Josie's fragile start in life was one of the most difficult things we had ever experienced, but as the weeks passed and she grew stronger and stronger, we

We older children help, encourage, and mentor our younger siblings—or sometimes a younger niece, as Joy-Anna enjoys doing with our niece, Mackynzie.

witnessed miracle after miracle as we saw how God used even Josie's premature life to touch many people and draw our family closer together.

When Mom and Daddy told us in summer 2011 that another baby was coming, we were so happy. And in December of that year we excitedly waited for them to come home after Mom's twenty-week ultrasound at her doctor's office. As soon as someone spotted their car coming down the driveway, we sounded the alarm (meaning, put out a call over the intercom) and hurried to greet them.

The night before, we had held a family meeting to vote on which first and middle names we liked the best. If the baby was a girl, then we girls would be celebrating that the Duggar tribe would finally be split evenly: ten girls and ten boys. If it was a boy, we would celebrate a happy change of nursery colors after the birth of four baby girls in a row.

Mom and Dad were pelted with eager questions as soon as they came through the door. Then, when we'd all settled down, Daddy said softly, "Mama . . ."

Mama smiled a sweet smile and said, as tears welled up in her eyes, "We had the ultrasound . . . and there was no heartbeat. Our baby has died."

We were stunned. Speechless. The baby brother or sister we had so looked forward to holding and playing with . . . was gone. There was no holding back the tears as Mom shared the story of how the technician had started the ultrasound, how she had looked and looked at the screen, how she had paused and turned to them, looking so sad, and said, "I'm so sorry."

The doctor had confirmed that there was no heartbeat, shared what comfort she could as a longtime family friend, and told them that Mom would probably go into labor sometime soon and deliver the stillborn baby.

As Christians, we believe that God can use everything that happens to us—even the hardest heartache—for good (see Romans 8:28), and in faith we thank God "in every thing" (1 Thessalonians 5:18). So we weren't at all surprised to have Dad tell us that one of the first things he and Mom did after hearing this devastating news was to pray together, thanking God for the weeks they had had with the baby as they happily anticipated the joy they would feel when they held the little one in their arms. They thanked Him for their unshakable faith that they would see that child someday in heaven. And then they asked the Lord for peace and for the strength they would need to go home and share the hard news with their other children.

Mom and Dad told us it's natural to weep and we shouldn't be ashamed of our tears. We all feel great sadness when we lose a loved one. They reminded us that we don't weep "as others which have no hope" (1 Thessalonians 4:13) because we know that one day we will see our sister in heaven. But we sadly miss her now.

A few days later Mom went into labor, and little Jubilee Shalom Duggar was born. Her name means "joyful celebration of peace." She had beautiful blue eyes, and a very cute little Duggar nose. She looked perfect in every way.

Our family held a memorial service for Jubilee a few days later, with close friends and family in attendance.

When Mama had announced she was pregnant with her twentieth child (actually it was her twenty-first, including a prior miscarriage more than twenty years ago), the news was reported in newspapers, magazines, and newscasts around the world. Now the headlines around the world reported Jubilee's passing, along with statements from our parents confirming that our little sister was loved. She was worth naming, worth having a memorial service for, and she would be missed.

In the months since then we have seen how God used Jubilee's short life and our big family's love-filled reaction to her death to remind people of the true value of life, born and unborn. We've also seen the value, again, of being a family of close relationships. When we go through challenging times of difficulty and change, God wants us to turn to Him and realize just how much we need Him. Our parents guided us through our grief over Jubilee's death in ways that helped us see that God is in control no matter what happens. Through the whole birth, burial, and grieving process, God drew us closer to Himself—and to each other. Those are just a few of the many ways God brought something good from what seemed to be a tragedy. Through Jubilee's passing, we have gained a greater appreciation for each sibling. The experience encouraged us to love each other even more, underscored our belief in the value of each life, and challenged us to take every opportunity to invest ourselves in each other, realizing we may not have tomorrow.

We grieved together when our baby sister, Jubilee Shalom, was stillborn, but we rejoice to know that, as Christians, we'll see her again someday in heaven. The display during her funeral, shown here, says, "There is no footprint too small that it cannot leave an imprint on this world."

4

Your Relationship with Friends

"Show me your friends, and I'll show you your future"

> *A man that hath friends must shew himself friendly:*
> *and there is a friend that sticketh closer than a brother.*
> —Proverbs 18:24

WE NEVER KNOW WHEN God is going to bring a new friend into our lives. One beautiful April morning as we were traveling to Big Sandy, Texas, to attend the annual Advanced Training Institute Family Conference, we had a tire blowout on the trailer we were pulling behind the RV. The trailer was packed with all the supplies we needed for a week of camping and attending the conference.

Dad and the boys were able to change the flat tire, but after examining some of the other tires, they decided we should probably go to a tire shop and buy a new spare. That meant going out of our way to find a tire store—a disappointment because we were all very eager to get to

Big Sandy and meet up with friends we hadn't seen since the last conference.

We ended up in a tire shop owned by a very sweet family that was also heading to the same homeschool conference later that day! What we first viewed as a setback turned out to be a huge blessing as we made some "accidental" new friends. We know now that God was orchestrating the whole thing.

The experience reinforced something Mom has taught us all our lives: that we are to thank God in *everything* He brings into our lives because we never know when a blessing, like a family of new friends, is waiting for us right around the bend—or in a small-town tire shop!

POINTING YOUR FRIENDS TO GOD

THE VERY BEST WAY to be a friend is to point your friends to Jesus. One powerful way we do this is by sharing testimonies of how God has worked in our own lives, just as our parents and Christian friends have shared their stories with us (see also Revelation 12:11). These stories help us understand how God can use any of us and anything—even our mistakes—to help others find their way to Him.

For example, Mom and Dad told us about a girl they knew—we'll call her Marie. Marie was fifteen and had a sweet personality and winsome ways that made her one of the most popular girls in her high school. Thin and beautiful, she was a girl every guy probably wished he could date.

But Mom told us those characteristics were all just outward appearances. Inside her heart, Marie battled intense insecurity, destructive thoughts and emotions, and a longing for "real" happiness. Somehow, the more popular she became, the stronger her desire for everyone's approval grew. And when she looked in the mirror, she didn't like what she saw—not her outward appearance or the inner feelings she wrestled with.

She was an active member of the gymnastics team, a key member of the cheerleading squad, and her classmates chose her as a homecoming attendant. But her discontentment with herself wouldn't go away. She constantly compared herself to others and was convinced she didn't measure up.

On the outside, Marie had what everyone else wanted, but on the inside, she felt sad and empty. She began to envy the girls who were thinner than she was, and she started believing that she would be happy if only she could be as thin as they were.

She heard about another girl who tried to control her weight through what turned out to be a destructive eating disorder. Not realizing how dangerous it was, Marie thought it might work for her, and soon her obsession to stay thin started controlling her life.

Meanwhile, Marie was consumed with comparing herself with others and constantly worrying about what they thought of her.

Then one night a girlfriend invited her to spend the night, and that friend shared with her a movie that portrayed the end of the world. The movie terrified Marie. When it finally ended, Marie told her friend how scared she felt about what would happen to her when she died. Marie's family didn't go to church, and she had never read the Bible.

Her friend told her that Christians don't have to be afraid of death or of the world ending, because they believe what the Bible says and they know they have the promise of eternal life in heaven.

Marie was amazed by her friend's fearless confidence. She didn't know what her friend was talking about, but she was very curious— and she wanted the same confidence she saw in her friend. So when the friend invited Marie to go to church with her the next night for a special revival service, Marie eagerly accepted.

During the church service, the preacher shared how God loves everyone, but that each person, individually, has violated His commandments. (At some point in our lives, we've all told a lie, taken something that's not ours, had lustful thoughts, etc.) He went on to explain that *that* is the reason God sent His Son, Jesus, to earth—to pay the penalty for *our* sins. Jesus was sinless, yet He took the punishment for what we have done wrong when He was executed on the cross.

Then the preacher went on to share that if we, in faith, believe in the Lord Jesus Christ and ask God the Father to forgive us for our sins as we turn from sin and give God the "steering wheel" of our life, He will come into our lives, guide us, give us peace, and take us to heaven when we die.

At the end of the service, the minister invited anyone who wanted to know more to come forward to speak with him. Marie popped out of her seat without an instant's hesitation and hurried to the front of the church. She talked with the pastor, and right then and there, she asked God to forgive her sins and committed herself to following God's plan for her life.

Marie joined an after-school club called Youth for Christ and started attending church occasionally. She got a job working at a yogurt shop and ended up falling in love with the shop manager's son. Not only did she enjoy his sense of humor and appreciate his thoughtful manners, but she was especially impressed by the young man's character and his love for the Lord. She'd never met anyone who had such a passion to seek after God. She found that passion contagious.

As they talked, Marie began to open up and eventually told the guy about her eating disorder. They prayed together frequently, and the two of them became accountability partners. With God's help, over the next few months Marie overcame her devastating eating issues.

She and the shop manager's son were married a few weeks after she graduated from high school; she was seventeen, and he was nineteen. They went on to have a houseful of children—nineteen, in fact, including four daughters they named Jana, Jill, Jessa, and Jinger . . .

The girl in the story was not actually named Marie, but Michelle. Now, Michelle Duggar. We call her Mom. And the boy she fell in love with? We call him Dad. Mom's story teaches us so many lessons. First, it shows how God can use anything and anyone to change another person's life for the better—something as "frivolous" as a high school student's overnight stay at a girlfriend's house or as unlikely as a teenage boy's boldness to talk about spiritual principles found in the Bible.

It also shows how God can work through hard times and difficult circumstances to draw a person closer to Himself and bring about a change in his or her life. Mom's teenage struggle for self-acceptance led her into some difficult emotional times and a very destructive habit that could have destroyed her health. But when her heart was opened to the gospel message and she received the truth that God loves us and that He wants to forgive us and offer us eternal life in heaven, then

Mom and Dad's first date, in May 1983. They dressed up for Dad's high school banquet.

she was able—with God's help and through strong accountability—to move away from the wrong choices she had made in her past.

Another lesson we've learned from Mom's story and from our own experience is the powerful influence one friend can be in another's life—for good or for bad. We think about the negative impact of Jessa's friend (in the chapter on "Your Relationship with Yourself") who was so focused on outward appearances and compare it to the life-changing impact Mom's teenage girlfriend had on Mom's life when they talked about life after death, and then when that friend invited Mom to church. That's the kind of impact we hope to have with our friends—wherever and however God chooses to use us.

LEARNING ABOUT BEING JUDGMENTAL

AND THAT LEADS US to one more story we hope will help you understand what it means to "grow up Duggar." It's about something that happened a while ago as most of our family was in a van headed to the store. As we passed a girl walking down the sidewalk, one of the little boys yelled, "Don't look! That girl's not dressed right!"

The girl was probably an older teenager, and she was wearing a short-short skirt and a rather low-cut top. Our little brother's tone was admittedly judgmental as he added, "That's really bad!"

Our family's tradition is that if we're walking down the street as a group and someone dressed inappropriately is coming toward us, one of us will quietly say, "Nike." That's a signal to the boys, and even to Dad, that they should nonchalantly drop their eyes and look down at their shoes as we walk past her. It's meant to help keep the guys' eyes from seeing things they shouldn't be seeing. By using the single-word signal, the warning can be given quietly and discreetly. We sure don't want to be judgmental of others.

But on this day as we drove by the girl on the sidewalk, our little brother shared his opinion in a style all his own. In response, Mom issued a gentle but unforgettable reminder. "Be very careful how you talk about others," she said. "I used to run around dressed worse than that."

The vanload of kids was quiet for a moment as Mom's words sank in. Then she added, "Not long ago, that was your mama."

And besides, she said, not everybody has the same standards.

Mom reminded us that when she was growing up, totally clueless about modesty, she used to mow her yard in a bikini—and she wondered why the neighbor lady didn't really like her (of course, the lady wanted to protect her husband and son from seeing the lawn girl)!

Some girls have a low self-worth, and they may think the only way they can attract a guy is to dress in a sensual way. But Mom says she was just naïve and no one had taken the time to explain to her what *modesty* meant. Back then she had no clue how her skimpy clothing affected guys around her.

It wasn't until after she became a Christian that she started re-evaluating how she dressed—and the other activities in her life as well, desiring to please God in every area. As a high school cheerleader dancing before a big crowd at a sporting event, she thought she was just getting everyone excited about the game. She had no idea that dancing around in a short skirt in front of a bunch of boys was causing many of them to think sensual thoughts about her and the other cheerleaders. When Mom began to understand this halfway through her senior year, she prayed about it and then decided to resign from the cheerleading squad. Since then she has always tried to dress modestly.

A lot of people didn't understand why she would choose to give up one of the most coveted positions in the high school, but that was where she felt God was leading her. She also used to go to school dances but stopped participating when God convicted her that dancing stirred up a lot of sensual desires in young men and women that could not be righteously fulfilled. These decisions were a huge step in the beginning of Mom's journey of trusting God. And her Christian walk began simply because a friend reached out to her and pointed her to Jesus.

BEING A FRIEND TO OTHERS

MOM HAS ALWAYS MODELED how a positive outlook, a cheerful disposition, and a friendly approach impact whatever situation we're in, whether something goes wrong when we're at home or in a stressful situation out on the road somewhere. We've seen how other people are drawn to Mom as though pulled in by a magnet. It's because of her constantly cheerful attitude and because she is always ready to give a friendly, encouraging word to everyone she meets. She has a genuine heart of gold. She has befriended many, many people around the world, and she daily models for us how a pleasant demeanor can be a blessing to everyone nearby.

Daddy shares a story of another woman whose personality had that kind of impact on the people around her. The woman was Betty, a cashier at the grocery store where Dad worked when he was in high school. He noticed that Betty always had the longest line of any of the store clerks. It always seemed that Betty would have four or five people waiting in her line even when there was no one else in the other checkout lanes.

At first Dad was puzzled—*I wonder why all these people want her to check out their groceries?* Then one day he figured it out. Betty genuinely loved and cared about others, and to her, the people in her checkout lane weren't simply customers. They had become her friends. She made it a point to remember her customers' names, and she would ask about their families and make a personal connection with each one of them, all while efficiently ringing up their groceries. Later, when they would come back through, she would remember something they had told her and ask how things were going. She didn't spend time talking about her own life or her problems but was always expressing interest in others.

Because of her winsome personality, customers loved her and were willing to wait in her lane just for a chance to say hello and share the latest news about their family or to update Betty on some other topics. Dad realized she was an amazing lady, and during the years he worked there, he learned a lot by just observing her work and interact with others.

We've seen this same lesson modeled by our parents again and again. And it's true: the person who shows love the most is loved the most! By asking friends questions about themselves, their interests, and their backgrounds, we let them know we care about them. That's the kind of friend everybody wants.

Dad has told us about Dorothy Dix, a very popular advice columnist in her time who reportedly wrote, "There is nothing you can possibly say to an individual that would be half as interesting to him as the things he is dying to tell you about himself. And all you need, in order to get the reputation of being a fascinating companion, is to say: 'How wonderful! Do tell me some more.'"

When Dad meets a new person, let's say it's a man he's sitting be-

Dad and Mom helped Johannah and Jackson at their Alex's Lemonade Stand Foundation booth to collect donations for cancer research.

side on an airplane, he will ask what kind of work he does, if he has children, where he lives, and where he grew up. And then Dad listens to the answers and responds in ways that say, "Tell me more!" He can carry on a ten-minute conversation simply by listening to answers to these questions. Then he will usually ask them questions about their church background, maybe starting with "Did you ever go to church anywhere growing up?"

His hope is to be a spiritual encouragement to those he comes in contact with. Often he will share a scripture from the Bible or possibly some of our favorite resources that have helped our family, such as the website embassyinstitute.org.

By taking a genuine, friendly interest in others, we can open doors to share about Jesus's love and point others to His Word.

Bringing up spiritual matters can feel somewhat awkward at first! But when you've shown you truly care for others, the questions come more naturally and usually are understood as concern rather than as judgment or criticism.

Our friend Andrew had one of those experiences that paid off in a huge way when he was talking to another friend, Nathan Bates. As the two young men were talking about what they wanted to do with their lives, Andrew mentioned that he might want to go into photography. Nathan told Andrew he should be praying and asking God what He wants him to do with his life. That got Andrew thinking, and after some soul searching, he realized he had never truly committed his life to God and that he was directing his own life.

Andrew ended up asking Jesus to come into his life and to be his Lord and Savior. Nathan then offered to disciple him to help him grow as a Christian; Nathan became his "accountability buddy." They both committed to start at the beginning of the Bible and read five chapters each day (knowing this would get them through the entire Bible in a year). Later Nathan invited our brother Joseph and a few other guys to join them in reading through the Bible. Each week Nathan would call up the guys individually to talk about what they had read and what they were learning. This grew into more than a dozen young men reading through the Bible together, and it had a huge impact on all of their lives.

Think about your last conversation with your friend. Did it lovingly challenge him or her spiritually?

Do your conversations tend to focus on a movie star you think is cute? A celebrity's latest romantic encounter? A classmate's messy breakup with her boyfriend? The shoes that girl in church was wearing? Or are they conversations that count for something? Ephesians 4:29 says, "Let no corrupt communication proceed out of your mouth, but that which is good to the use of edifying, that it may minister grace unto the hearers."

Many teenagers and young adults spend most of their time, energy, and thought focused on their friends and how they can have fun together. But think about the good you could do if your friendship focused not just on having fun right now but on matters of great importance—now and throughout eternity. We encourage you to carefully consider who you spend time with and what you do with that time. Jesus did not say to make friends but to make disciples!

STANDING ALONE

EVERYONE MAKES BAD CHOICES at times throughout life and ends up suffering the consequences for his or her actions. That's why it's so important to read the Bible and ask God what things He wants you to add to your life and what things He wants you to leave out. Predetermining what God wants you to leave out or add to your life is another way to describe *standards* or *convictions*. If you have strong convictions about what God wants you to do (or not do), then when you're faced with a situation where friends ask you to do something, you can run it through the filter of God's Word to know what He thinks about it. Living your life based on what you believe God's Word says can sometimes mean not fitting in with the crowd, but in the long run, you will have avoided the pitfalls that have destroyed many young people's lives. We should not judge one another or try to force our beliefs on others, but it doesn't hurt to discuss what the Bible says about different topics to encourage each other in our walk with God.

One of the most important demonstrations of character and integrity comes when a person has the courage to stand for what he or she knows is right—even when that means standing alone.

One of the stories Mom and Dad have told us kids repeatedly is about a couple whose young daughter begged her parents to let her go to an overnight slumber party at one of her classmates' homes. She felt this was a big deal, and all the other girls in her class were going to be there. The parents checked out the invitation and talked to the parents of the slumber party girl and decided to let their daughter go. But before her dad dropped her off, he talked to her about the importance of standing alone.

Jinger and Dad enjoyed our sightseeing flight over the Grand Canyon, but the scenery inside the little plane wasn't so pretty. Most of us got really airsick.

He told her, "If someone ever asks you to do something you know is wrong, you can say politely, 'I've given my life to Jesus, and I'm not able to do that.'" He prayed with her before she got out of the car, asking Jesus to make her a positive influence while she was with the other girls and also that she would have the courage to stand up for what was right.

The party was lots of fun, and the girl had a great time playing games with her friends. And of course, what is a birthday party without a big piece of cake and a scoop of vanilla ice cream? But late that night, before bed, the mom suggested they have a "pretend séance" using a Ouija board.

When the girl heard what this involved, she said respectfully and quietly to the group, "I'm not going to be able to do this."

When the mom asked why not, the girl replied, "I've given my life to Jesus, and I'm not able to do things like this."

The mother was stunned by the little girl's words—and by her quiet courage in speaking up for her beliefs. She packed up the Ouija board and suggested the girls play something else before bed.

Our parents have told us this story many times, and as youngsters we role-played how we would respond to friends who suggested doing something we knew we shouldn't do.

We all face times when someone—many times even a friend—might encourage us to do something we know we shouldn't do. It's essential to understand how to stand firm on what you know to be the truth, especially when it comes to something that would contradict God's Word.

Sometimes Christians have to stand up for their own beliefs and convictions even when they're with other Christians. This is much harder because, all too often, it will be fellow Christians who give us the hardest time over our differences. Other Christians sometimes assume that just because we choose to do or not do something we are judging them for not being exactly like us. That's not the case! We realize that God leads people and that not everybody will embrace the same things or at the same time.

For example, some friends of ours had a husband and wife visiting at their house one day, and one of the kids suggested that this man join them for a card game—probably something like Speed or Spoons. But their friend politely refused. The kids thought that was unusual, but later the man explained that his father had been a gambler who had wasted away all the family savings, gambling on card games. As a result, the man had vowed that he would never touch a deck of playing cards. It was his personal conviction.

Sometimes when we see someone else's convictions as offbeat, we may be tempted to try to talk that person out of something we see as silly or unnecessary. But this man's story reminds us that God may have put that conviction in place for a specific reason, as a safeguard or protection. We should never make fun of others' standards.

ENCOURAGING FRIENDS TO DO RIGHT

OUR PARENTS HAVE OCCASIONALLY cautioned us about a person who could be a bad influence, and they've given us ideas for how we might encourage him or her toward wiser decisions. Sometimes it's amazing to see what just a few words can do to help someone reevaluate what he or she is doing; in the same way, simple words can encourage someone to grow in his or her walk with the Lord.

This is true even for the youngest children. Dad became a Christian when he was only seven, and one day when he and some other little grade school classmates were out on the playground, one of the boys started using God's name as a curse word. Dad quietly told the boy he wished he wouldn't misuse God's name. "After all," Dad told his little friend, "He's the One who made us and loves us."

From then on, when Dad was playing with these boys and a bad word slipped out, they would catch themselves and apologize. They really tried to think about the words they were saying. He and Mom have shown us that sometimes it's good to speak up politely and respectfully in situations where something happens that we know is wrong—especially with our Christian friends—and to encourage them to do what is right.

If it's true that the negative peer pressure of a friend is the greatest motivation to do wrong, then the opposite would also be true: positive peer pressure is the greatest motivation to do right. There will be times when, as a loving friend, we may need to bring it to someone's attention that something he or she did or said has hurt or offended another person. Just as we discussed when we were talking about sibling relationships, in Matthew 18 Jesus gives us a proper way for handling offenses one-on-one, and it does not include blabbing gossip to other friends.

One of the things that destroys relationships with friends and siblings almost faster than anything else is mean-spirited teasing and joking. And often, this is another situation that calls for you to speak up or confront a friend. Now, we've already said that Duggars are the first to enjoy a laugh as a family when everyone involved knows

that something is a joke and it doesn't belittle or hurt anyone. And by now you probably understand that Daddy loves nothing more than pulling a good joke on someone. (Remind us sometime to tell you about the time, after a meal in a foreign country, Dad convinced some of us, including an unsuspecting family friend, that he'd found out the meat in the entrée we'd just eaten was barbecued dog.)

Here's Dad around age seven or eight. Even at a young age, he stood up for what is right.

But remember: it's important that the joke *doesn't* involve teasing, where someone is ridiculed for something he or she did either accidentally or on purpose (we should never "jokingly" call anyone names or put others down).

Mom and Dad have stressed to us from an early age that making fun of someone is *never* right.

Mom tells us about an incident during her high school days when she overheard some football players teasing another student, daring him to eat a bug and jeering that he wasn't tough enough to do it. He wanted the football players' acceptance so much that he finally popped the bug into his mouth and took a few chews. But as soon as he swallowed it, they ridiculed him even more, making fun of him and telling him he was disgusting for doing something "so gross."

Mom was a cheerleader at the time, and she charged into the crowd of bullies and chewed them out for being so mean. It makes us laugh now to think of our sweet mama bawling out those big, tough football guys who probably towered over her. But she wasn't about to stand by while someone was badly mistreated.

In this case, the offense was done by multiple people and it was being carried out publicly, so Mom jumped on their unkind behavior right in the middle of the situation. Usually, though, we would try to take that person aside and "tell him his fault between thee and him alone," as Jesus tells us to do in Matthew 18:15.

UNDERSTANDING THE IMPACT OF A FRIENDSHIP

MOM AND DAD HAVE taught us to understand how influential friends can be for good or bad, and they've stressed the importance of choosing friends wisely. They have said that, just like a ship has a small rudder that determines its direction, our friendships and our small choices determine our life direction.

Earlier in this book we described how I (Jessa) had friends whose attention, as we grew into the teenage years, seemed to be constantly focused on temporal things and outward appearances—such as which girls had the prettiest hair and cutest clothes and which ones didn't. The more I was around them, the more I found myself forming that perspective on life as well.

It's especially easy for teenage girls to get caught up in this kind of thing at a time when what we want most is to be accepted by others. But my parents helped me put those friends' attitudes in perspective. I became determined to find friends who helped me focus on character, such as having a kind, servant-hearted attitude toward others, instead of friends whose focus was fixed on watching all the newest movies, listening to the latest pop music, and judging others whom they deemed "not cool."

True friends encourage us to focus on things that are beneficial to us. We will grow closer to God because of our relationship with them. We share an interest in reading and memorizing Scripture and learning more about living a Christ-like life. We enjoy working together to serve others whether it's on a mission trip to Central America or helping an elderly neighbor clean up and maintain a deteriorating home. We can share our struggles with godly friends, knowing they will keep what we say in confidence and give advice for wise decisions based on God's Word.

Our Grandma Duggar's story shows how one person, striving to live this kind of life, can have a powerful impact on others. Grandma grew up in a very poor family. Her home didn't have indoor plumbing or air-conditioning. A wood-burning stove in their small home's living room provided the only heat in wintertime.

When Grandma was fifteen, she became a Christian, but the rest of her family didn't go to church. In fact, for several years, one of her brothers would mock her and make fun of her faith in God. Her dad was a very angry man who often used foul language. Her mom worked long hours in a chicken-processing plant. It was a hard life.

Grandma Duggar is an important part of our family—and also a great miniature golfer, as Justin, Jason, and Josiah can attest.

However, despite her very difficult situation, Grandma Duggar's faith in God grew stronger as she continued to attend church, read her Bible regularly, and do what God's Word said to do. She didn't "preach" to her family. She simply and quietly modeled a Christlike life for them.

Years later, her younger sister and her brother, who had been self-proclaimed atheists, ended up becoming Christians. The brother who used to mock her is now a Sunday school teacher. Grandma kept the faith despite her family's apathy and opposition, and in doing so she became a light God used in drawing her loved ones to Himself.

We want friends like that: those who will not only "talk the talk" about what they believe but also "walk the walk," living out their beliefs in everyday life and working to follow what God says even when the going gets tough. It's such a blessing to have friends who have that genuine enthusiasm for the Lord. We're happy to have *that* kind of influence rub off on us! And that's also the kind of friend we should strive to be.

On the other hand, we want to be careful about the people with whom we choose to share our time and our hearts as close companions. An incident in one of our family's rental properties a few years ago served as an illustration for the way prolonged contact with a corrosive influence can cause harm, even when it seems unlikely. The situation occurred after Dad rented a commercial warehouse to a local soda distributor. When the renter decided he no longer needed the space, he agreed with Dad that he would leave a few things behind to cover the remaining money owed. Included in the things left behind there were a few pallets of sugarcane sodas plus a large pallet of energy drinks.

We shared some of the drinks with friends, but there were too many to get through right away. When the weather changed dramatically, a couple of the cases of energy drinks exploded. But the problem wasn't noticed for a couple of weeks, and by then the sugary, carbonated liquid had had plenty of time to soak into the floor. When the guys began the cleanup process, spraying down the floor with a pressure washer, they were shocked to find that the energy drinks had actually *eroded away a layer of the concrete*—in some places, a half-inch deep!

Mom made a parallel out of the situation and pointed out to us how the same thing happens when we spend lots of time with "friends" who may seem sweet and appealing but who are exerting a harmful influence on our hearts.

Dad has told us the story of a nice, likable young man who grew up in a Christian home but eventually became a drug addict. During this guy's high school years, he formed his closest friendships with a group of young people who had little character and would throw parties almost every weekend. Their sole purpose in life was to "have a good time." This young man had never been the wild type, but for whatever reason, he had begun to desire their acceptance.

One night when he was invited to a party by one of these friends, he decided to go. Seeing that he was a bit standoffish at first and in the corner by himself, his friend walked by and handed him a beer. Now he had a decision to make (and obviously, he never should have put himself in this situation in the first place).

This guy had grown up in church, so he knew the Bible has a lot to say about the foolishness of drinking alcohol (see Proverbs 20:1 and Proverbs 23:29–35). At first he just stood there holding the beer in his hand, smiling and contemplating what he would do. He had never had a desire to drink, but he did not want to feel like an outsider, so when no one was looking he poured half the beer into a nearby potted plant. A little later his friend came by and said, "You didn't drink any, did you?" Then, grabbing the bottle out of his hand, he noticed that it was half empty. "Hey, guys, he's one of us!" the friend announced to everyone.

Shortly after that the young man started drinking; later he got introduced to drugs. How sad that one, seemingly small decision started him on a path of self-destruction. If only he would have looked down the road and counted the cost! Instead, he lived only for the moment, and it ruined his life.

Proverbs 24:1–2 warns, "Be not thou envious against evil men, neither desire to be with them. For their heart studieth destruction, and their lips talk of mischief."

Mom tells of another young man she knew who was a top honor student. Because of his intellectual genius, he received a full four-year scholarship to the University of Arkansas. But he formed friendships with the wrong people. Every Sunday morning he was in church, but every Friday and Saturday night he was out drinking with his friends. One weekend he was involved in an alcohol-related rollover accident, and it nearly took his life. He survived, but he ended up suffering brain damage that permanently changed the course of his future. My parents have often wondered what his life would have been like had he made other choices.

By hearing these examples, we Duggars have seen the importance of choosing friends who will encourage us to do right and make wise decisions. But we're definitely not talking about living in a bubble and refusing to have contact with those who are not Christians or don't believe just the way we do. In fact, as Christians, our purpose in life is just the opposite. We're to reach out to everyone in love, sharing a kind word or a helping hand, no matter what a person's beliefs or background. But in these interactions, it's important to stand strong and not be swayed by others' beliefs. While it's good to minister to others, we need to make sure at the same time that we are not carelessly walking into situations where we're going to be tempted to make wrong choices.

Dad uses this analogy quite often: Imagine you're standing on a table, trying to pull someone up. You have to be very careful, because many times the other person can pull you down a lot easier than you can pull that person up! But if there were two people on the table, it would be much harder for *both* of them to be pulled down, and together they would have a much better chance of helping the other person up onto the table. Keeping this in mind, when we are ministering

Several of us enjoyed biking in Central Park during a visit to New York City.

to a person in need, we Duggars often work two-on-one, just to have that extra encouragement and "the upper hand."

A true friend is one who spiritually encourages us and motivates us to do what is right, rather than undermining our beliefs. We should all strive to be that kind of friend to others.

One of the easiest ways to form this kind of friendship is to spend time with people who are growing spiritually and who have a ministry mind-set. Good Christian friends may or may not be part of the "in crowd," but it's much more important to have friends who love God deeply and want to serve Him than to have friends who are concerned about popularity, status, and recognition!

The best place to find this type of friend is at a Bible-teaching church. Search out those who are excited about the things of God and spend time with them. It will be contagious!

As Grandma Duggar always says, "Show me your friends, and I'll show you your future."

When you look at the people you've chosen as friends, what kind of future do you see?

5

YOUR RELATIONSHIP WITH GUYS

Saving yourself for the one God has for you

*Let no man despise thy youth; but be thou an example of the believers,
in word, in conversation, in charity, in spirit, in faith, in purity.*
—1 Timothy 4:12

NEW from Jill and Jessa . . .

WE WROTE THE ORIGINAL version of this book before any of us were married—even before we were officially courting. But now that two of us have gone through the courting process and are happily married (but still have lots to learn!), we wanted to share some of our experiences with you. We know that no couple goes through the courting process in exactly the same way as another couple, but we thought you might like to know how we navigated courtship, and we hope you will find some principles that will guide you in your relationship with guys.

OUR PARENTS HAVE ALWAYS said marriage is the most special gift from God next to salvation. Even after the many exciting years and struggles of raising nineteen kids and counting, they are still deeply in love and committed to each other. They made a lifelong vow to God to stick together until "death do us part."

When Mom and Dad were married on July 21, 1984, they were both really young. Mom was seventeen, and Dad was nineteen. Their marriage from the beginning was focused on sharing God's love with others.

Mom and Dad have said there are two main keys to maintaining a strong marriage.

1. Being willing to say "I was wrong."
2. And asking "Will you please forgive me?"

They also have committed to never go to bed angry but to make things right in the day an offense happens.

Mom and Dad's engagement picture, 1984.

We have seen the blessings of a God-centered marriage through our parents' example, and all of us do desire to one day marry. But simply getting married quickly just to *be* married isn't a goal for us. We want to wait for the one God has created for us and get married in His timing.

Our family gets a lot of letters and e-mails with questions about our family's beliefs and practices related to marriage—or, more accurately, to the process we prefer to follow leading up to marriage. We call it courtship—or dating with a purpose—and that's something we'll discuss in this chapter.

FULFILLING THE CRAVING TO BE LOVED

ABOUT THE TIME WE entered our teenage years, Dad told us a story about a girl he went to school with in elementary and junior high school who was boy-crazy. He said she would have a boyfriend for a week or so, and then something would happen and she would get upset and break it off with him. Then, a few days later, she would have a new boyfriend, and then she would switch to another, then another.

Dad said this cycle went on for years. (No, our dad was never one of her many boyfriends!) He said he wondered at that early age if eventually this girl would find Mr. Right or if her habit of throwing herself into relationship after relationship would prove to be preparation for a future unstable marriage.

Sadly enough, when this girl finally got married, it didn't last long, and that same pattern of discontent, insecurity, and self-centeredness that had affected her dating also affected her marriage.

We have met some girls who have simply fallen in love with the idea of marriage and are just looking for a guy to fulfill their dreams. They have an image in mind of what marriage is, and they are in love with that image. One girl told us recently, "I was in love with the thought of being in love, and it consumed my every waking hour." This is one of the greatest dangers of romance novels. They paint a picture of an unrealistic, unobtainable relationship. It's the same thing pornography does to men. Viewing pornography gives them a distorted view of women that leads them down the path of immorality and guilt.

Perhaps the biggest problem with pornography is that it never satisfies and instead creates an unrealistic expectation of what a woman's body looks like. No woman can live up to these Photoshopped and airbrushed images because they are not real. And no man addicted to pornography will ever be content with a real woman because the woman he's looking for does not exist.

Men who feed their minds on pornography start looking at women as sex objects to fulfill their out-of-control desires instead of looking at women as someone to be protected, loved, and cared for. They become self-centered, and when they start a relationship, their focus is on what they can get out of it instead of what they can put into it. This mind-set eventually leads to the destruction of what could have been a fulfilling marriage.

How horrible! No girl would want to be married to that kind of husband. And yet when a girl reads romance novels, she's doing something very similar, drawing perfectionistic, romantic pictures into her mind of what she thinks marriage is. Soon she's longing for this "ideal" marriage that she has created in her mind, and she does everything she can to get it.

So many girls look to boys and marriage to give them what only God can give: satisfaction, security, happiness, fulfillment, and lasting significance. Girls must realize that no man can ever give them these things 100 percent of the time. Even the best men will mess up, and if we're relying on them to be perfect, we will become bitter and disillusioned when they don't measure up.

It's important to understand that God created us with an inborn need to be accepted and loved. If you're a living, breathing person, you want someone to share your day, your passions, your desires, and the depths of your heart. But the truth is, marriage itself cannot make you truly happy. God put that deep need to be loved and accepted in our hearts so that *He* could be the One to fulfill it.

When you look to marriage for what only God can give, you make an idol out of marriage. The dictionary definition of *idolatry* is "an extreme admiration, love, or reverence for something or someone." Boys, marriage, and love can become idols.

~⟳

NEW from Jill . . .

NOT LONG AFTER DERICK and I were married, we had some high school girls in our home. One of the girls asked us, "How's married life?" Derick and I shared that it's great and that we are so happy to be together.

However, Derick cautioned her: "At this point in your life, you need to be content with where God has you."

"But," she enthusiastically responded, "I just can't wait to get married and have a relationship like yours."

We understood how she felt, but encouraged her not to be absorbed in the future. What she needs to do now is be the godly girl that a godly guy is looking for. I encouraged her to focus on serving God rather than trying to get a guy's attention. It's easy for girls to get consumed with thoughts of marriage. Then they try to be the "perfect" person and soon get discouraged. The Bible calls us to be content in whatever situation we're in (Philippians 4:12). If you're not content outside of marriage, you won't be content in marriage, either.

~⟳

GOD WANTS US TO have a wholehearted relationship with Him, delighting in His Word and all that He has to teach us. When we understand that He is trustworthy and faithful and that He alone knows our every need, then we know where to look for deep love and full acceptance.

When we have this kind of close, loving relationship with our Creator, we can experience a joy and fulfillment that would be completely missed if our lives were consumed merely with finding our Prince Charming.

I (Jill) took advantage of every opportunity before we were married to take a chaperone or two and have lunch with Derick at work.

This also means that someday, when we do meet the man God intends as our husband, we'll already be fulfilled, and any love that future husband gives us is a bonus over what we're already receiving from our relationship with the Lord.

As teenagers and young adults, we need to cherish these single years when we are able to put our focus on serving God and use this time to its fullest. Mom has told us older kids many times, "If God gives you a full, seventy-year life, your time as a single person is very short compared with the time you're married. Be content with every stage of life and wherever God has you; use your time wisely and invest in things that will last for eternity."

Her words remind us to use these single years wisely as a time that can be fun, exciting, and fruitful with opportunities to teach younger girls, serve the elderly, volunteer in the community, go on mission trips, and seek out ways to bless others through ministry. These years should be devoted, first and foremost, to strengthening and solidifying our relationship with God and understanding who He is and who He has created us to be.

NEW from Jessa . . .

WHEN BEN AND I first started courting, Ben was a wonderful example of using his single years to become the man God wanted him to be. Ben was working at a golf course as part of the lawn care crew, and he had to get up at 4 A.M. to get to work on time. He would use his drive to work as a time to pray and worship God through singing songs of

praise. Throughout the day as he
went about his mowing and such,
he would put in his earbuds and listen to sermons. He introduced me
to www.sermonaudio.com. As he listened to great messages from men
like Charles Spurgeon, Voddie Bau-
cham, and Paul Washer, he would
text me a link so I could hear it, too.

Best friends! ♥

We still do this to this day! I love this about him! These godly men are
his heroes. These are the kind of men he looks up to and wants to be
like. I'm thankful to God that Ben used those single years to mature
in his faith.

Our family definitely keeps busy and experiences all kinds of different rides, but
riding camels in Israel was something we never expected to get to do. It was fun!

DEFINING THE PURITY RING

THIS DOESN'T MEAN WE'RE to ignore the fact that God has created us to have a natural physical desire toward men. When these feelings arise, we thank God for making us "normal." Within a godly marriage, this kind of desire can be a wonderful blessing that bonds the husband and wife together in the way God intended. But during our single years, this physical attraction, if not carefully controlled, can also be one of the biggest sources of temptation and struggles.

One way our parents have helped us understand the principles designed to keep us pure is by giving all of us older girls purity rings. The rings were special gifts we received when the four of us were in our early teenage years (because our family didn't become aware of this relatively new practice until then). Mama selected some very special rings from her jewelry box for each of us to choose from. Jana's ring has one red sapphire surrounded by tiny diamonds. Jill's is a beautiful pearl. Jinger's ring has a heart design set with a small diamond. Jessa's is a beautiful solid yellow gold band.

To each of us, the ring has a fourfold purpose. First, it's a symbol of our commitment to keep ourselves physically pure as we wait for the one God intends for us to marry. Second, it symbolizes our desire to involve our parents in our decision of a life partner. Third, our ring reminds us to pray for the man God would have us marry and to guard our own heart so that one day we can share it fully with him. Fourth (and most important), it's a reminder that God is the true fulfiller of all our desires and also a reminder to cherish our relationship with Him and live purposefully between now and the time He sees fit to bring that man into our lives.

A few years ago, about the time our younger sister Joy was turning twelve, Mom and Dad prepared a special time when they could help Joy celebrate her entry into womanhood. Mama got Joy some special gifts—makeup and other girly things—and talked with her about the changes she was going through. She told her she wasn't a little girl anymore and that the physical and emotional changes she was starting to have are completely normal—a part of the change from girlhood to womanhood.

Then she and Dad went shopping with Joy to select her purity ring, and afterward they went to lunch together, and Dad explained that the purity ring symbolized her decision to keep herself pure and wait for the one God has for her. Meanwhile, they discussed how she could prepare herself during this time as a growing young lady to become the kind of woman a godly guy would desire to marry.

Dad has asked us girls, "What kind of girl do you think a godly guy will be attracted to?"

The answer is, a godly girl. That's what he and Mom are continually encouraging each of us girls to become. We know that a godly girl is not someone who has lived a "perfect" life but is someone who has received God's forgiveness and is seeking to put the past behind her and choosing to live every day for Him. Some of the greatest people in the Bible were those who had made a lot of bad decisions earlier in their life, but then God got a hold of them, and they completely turned over the rest of their life to following and serving Him.

FIGHTING TEMPTATION

MANY TIMES, PEOPLE, ESPECIALLY teenagers and young adults, confuse love with sensual desire. It might even be called *lust,* an urge based not on genuine love but on feelings, emotions, and a desire for pleasure. If a girl allows herself to be consumed with sensual desires, most likely she will attract a guy with the same wrong desires. These attractions may have little to do with character or godliness; instead, they're usually based solely on a person's looks and his or her witty or "flirty" personality. These relationships are based on nothing more than sensual attraction. They are usually short-lived and often result in great emotional pain and heartache.

A test of *lust* versus *true love* is that lust can never wait to get, but love can always wait to give. It is important to wait for the one God has for you and to wait for His timing to bring you together.

Sometimes it's easy to start dreaming, *Could he be the one?* when first meeting a guy without knowing his character or really anything about him. And if a girl becomes jealous or angry when the guy she likes starts a relationship with another gal, their relationship was not genuine love. Genuine love says, "I want him to marry the one God has for him, even if that means it isn't me."

~~~

NEW from Derick . . .

ONE OF THE GREATEST things I learned from other Christian guys is not to awaken the intimacy area of your life until the time is right. Don't put yourself in a position of getting close to a girl until you're ready to marry. And don't try to be with someone just to have someone to be with. It sets you up for failure. I would highly encourage you that if you don't see yourself being ready for marriage within the next year, don't pursue a girl during that time. If you aren't ready for a marriage relationship in the foreseeable future, then pursue the things that will prepare you for that part of your life—such as education, ministry, career, etc. Once Jill and I decided we wanted to get married, we also decided to have a short engagement and set ourselves up for success.

~~~

IF A GIRL GETS emotionally attached to a guy and can't wait for him to pop the question but feels she has to push him along, she should remember, *True love waits.* If it's God's will, He will work things out in His time. When we say true love waits, we mean that couples should not act like they're married when they're not or share physical intimacies that married couples share. Also, it's important to never consider living together until you're married, as this is clearly not God's will. If a guy is pressuring a girl to live with him or to experience things that are meant to be experienced only in marriage, that's not true love; it's lust. True love waits.

NEW from Jill . . .

WHILE I WAS GOING through my "waiting" time as a teenager, I went through some serious spiritual struggles and had to rely on God to control my thought life. There were times when fears and bad thoughts popped into my mind. I also struggled with comparing myself with others. When I shared these temptations with my parents, Mom asked me, "Who do you think put those thoughts in your head?" They explained how from the beginning of time Satan has used the same tactics on people over and over again to damage their lives and relationships with others. My parents had taught me to fight temptation by being ready with a prayer target every time Satan tempted me, so that's what I did. One of my prayer targets was a certain unsaved relative and the other was my future husband. Sometimes I'd be praying for my future husband and I'd say, "I don't know what he's going through, but please encourage him to be strong in his relationship with you, Lord, and especially in this area that I am struggling in right now."

After Derick and I began our courtship, I told him about my prayers for my future husband. A puzzled look came over his face, and he asked, "When was that?" I told him it was when I was fifteen or sixteen. "That's the time my dad died. It was a really hard time for me." Without even knowing Derick, I had been praying for him during one of his most difficult times, and those prayers not only helped him, but they helped me overcome Satan's temptation. Sometimes God uses the difficult things in our lives to benefit someone else. He sure did that with Derick and me.

⁓

OUR PARENTS HAVE BEEN a huge help to us in all areas of our lives, but their counsel has been especially valuable as we sort through the issues related to becoming a woman and as accountability partners when we are having struggles or going through a challenging time. It's important that we seek counsel from our parents (or another trusted adult) because we know they love us and want only what is best for our lives.

If one of us Duggars is struggling with any kind of temptation, we share it with our parents. Mom will wisely ask us, "Who do you think put that thought into your head?"

We know the answer is Satan. Our parents have stressed that it's not a sin on our part if Satan randomly throws an impure thought into our heads, but it *is* a sin to dwell on the temptation. Don't send yourself on a guilt trip because you're being tempted.

It's freeing to know that as long as we're not bringing these struggles on ourselves by actively pursuing things we shouldn't or having a curiosity for things we shouldn't, we are not in the wrong. It's what we do with this wrong thought from the devil that determines whether we are sinning. Dwelling on it *is* a sin, and it can lead us to give in to the wrong desires they create.

Dad says you can't do anything about the birds that fly in the sky above your head, but you can do something about a bird building a

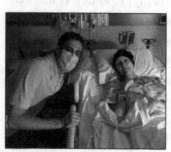

A lot of our (Jill's) wedding planning during our engagement was done in the hospital, while visiting Derick's mom, Cathy.

nest on top of your head. In the Bible, Paul talks of taking every thought captive. Basically this means being able to control what's going on in our mind. By censoring our thoughts through the filter of God's Word, we will be able to recant any wrong thoughts or temptations that try to sneak in, and throw out the lies the devil is sending our way.

One of the things Jana and I (Jill) learned during our firefighter training is that the quicker you respond to a dangerous fire, the less likely it is to cause serious damage. The same thing happens when we quickly respond to a "fire" sparked by a sinful thought that pops into our heads. Dad gave us a great idea for a quick response when tempted: he suggested we immediately use that as reminder to pray for someone else who needs God's help. We talked about this idea of having a "prayer target" in chapter 2. In this way, what Satan means for evil, we use as a reminder to do good. We like to think of it as a live hand grenade coming our direction, and before it explodes we quickly pick it up and throw it right back at the devil.

Satan has been recycling the same basic

When our older brother John-David completed training to become a volunteer with our local fire department, Jill, shown here, and Jana decided to volunteer, too.

temptations for the past six thousand years, but since he is the master deceiver, he tries to deceive us into thinking we're the only ones who struggle with the wrong thoughts or desires he sends our way. In reality, the temptation to lie, steal, cheat, bully, gossip, and think wrong thoughts has been around since the first couple, Adam and Eve, gave in to temptation in the Garden of Eden. The problem of temptation and sin has continued to the present day, which means your parents probably faced many of the same problems you're facing now, right down to the problem of feeling all alone and thinking your parents don't understand.

They understand a lot more than you may think they do. They understand that this time in life can be very intense—because they undoubtedly went through similar struggles when they were your age. They know about the many physical and social changes you're experiencing, including the wrong thoughts and other temptations Satan will put into your head.

Another bit of good news is that, as Christians, we're assured that God will not allow into our lives more temptation than we can bear. First Corinthians 10:13 says, "There hath no temptation taken you but such as is common to man: but God is faithful, who will not suffer you to be tempted above that ye are able; but will with the temptation also make a way to escape, that ye may be able to bear it."

Even though sometimes it seems a temptation is just too strong for us, we can overcome it if we receive the grace God offers. Because "with men this is impossible, but with God all things are possible" (Matthew 19:26). God will provide a way to escape temptations, and one way He does that is by providing parents or other trusted adults who understand what we're going through and can provide insights, encouragement, and guidance.

This is key when we're struggling in any area of life because Satan's power to keep us making the same mistakes is based in the secrecy of our sin. When secrets are brought to the light and we make ourselves accountable, it's much easier to find victory. All things start in the mind and grow into actions, and there's almost nothing our human mind won't try to rationalize away. But God's law is written on our hearts, and we still have a conscience that convicts us when we do wrong. It's vital that we learn how to have victory over temptations because continuing down that wrong path will only lead to trouble and heartache.

You may feel that right now your parents don't understand you and your turbulent thoughts and feelings, but we urge you to give them a chance! Ask them for help; ask them for advice. Be honest and open with them about what's on your mind and what you're walking through.

If you have already gone through a devastating trial from a past relationship or other wrong decisions, we want you to know that our Creator is a God of forgiveness and grace. If you turn from your sins, ask Him to forgive you, and commit your life to following Him, He will make you a new person and give you His desires, His dreams, and His goals for your life. Then guard your heart carefully against future intrusions of lust and instead fulfill your natural need for love and acceptance with the boundless love of God.

Romans 13:14 says to "make not provisions for the flesh, to fulfill the lusts thereof." That means we're to avoid (or stop) reading romance novels, teen magazines, and watching TV shows and movies that will stir up these sensual drives. Also, don't put yourself in a situation where you're alone with a guy, because bad things can happen. If you're in a relationship right now with someone who does not have a spiritual focus, talk to him about the importance of centering your relationship on God and waiting on the physical components until marriage. If he's not interested, ask God to help you let go.

If you stick with someone who spiritually is like a dead horse, you will hinder God's work in his life and your own. Grandma Duggar has always said, "Many girls think they can alter a guy at the marriage altar," and then she adds, "very rarely does that work! If a guy is not a spiritual leader before you marry him, marrying him will not change him."

～

NEW from Jessa . . .

AT THE VERY BEGINNING of our courtship, Ben and I decided that we wanted to outline very clear physical boundaries for this stage of our relationship. When it comes to temptations, the Bible tells us to stand strong and fight against them. But when it comes to sexual sin, we are told to *flee*. No standing and fighting—the Bible commands us to run! 1 Corinthians 6:18 tells us clearly to "flee fornication." The best way to protect yourself against sexual sin is to stay away from situations where you will be the most tempted.

Being alone together will always bring you the greatest temptations. Sin thrives in secrecy. It's just that simple. So when Ben and I would get together, we would hang out in the main parts of the house. Usually we would sit on the couch in our living room or at our dining room table. Our goal was to be within eyesight of other family members, but this did not mean we always had to be within earshot. Oftentimes, we wanted to talk and have conversations between just the two of us. Sometimes if the weather was nice, we'd sit on the front porch where others could see us through the window, and if we wanted to go on a date, we'd take a chaperone with us.

We sometimes get pushback on our physical guidelines.

"That's unromantic!" some protest.

"No, that's a safeguard!" we reply.

Others might say, "We don't struggle like that. We are strong! We wouldn't think of having sex before marriage."

We would have to caution you to take heed! You may be nearer to sin now than you have ever been before. In 1 Corinthians

10:12, the Apostle Paul warns, "Wherefore let him who thinks he stands take heed lest he fall." When you think yourself strong, you may just be at your weakest.

Happy courting couple!

Other people protest by asking, "Didn't your parents raise you right? Didn't they teach you right from wrong? Don't you trust yourselves to do the right thing?"

The answers are "Yes," "Yes," and "No."

We are all sinners. Till the day we die, we will have a sin nature inside of us that pulls us to do things we should not. It would be a serious error to think we are strong enough to resist physical temptation when we allow ourselves to be alone and unaccountable.

Yes, it's true that when we are tempted by the devil, God gives us a way to escape. But all too often, we practically invite temptation into our lives. It's like we climb into a small boat, paddle out miles into the dangerous sea, and then begin drilling holes in the bottom of our boat. Then, when our vessel has sunk and we are miles out from the safety of shore, we wonder, "How did I get here? How did this happen?" If we'll look down, we'll see the drill in our hand. The devil cannot take all the blame. Sometimes, self is the culprit, and God's way of escape was long since passed by.

NEW from Derick and Jill . . .

Derick: JILL AND I had a mutually beneficial relationship with our chaperones. What I mean by this is that they helped us and we helped them. Their help was in the form of giving us someone to be accountable to, and our help to them was in the form of "thank-yous"—like pizza, candy, gift cards, etc. Our chaperones were mainly friends and family who were older than eleven or twelve. James and Joy were our most-used chaperones. We even made a spreadsheet showing what each chaperone liked. We also tried to include them in what we were doing. If we wanted to study together at Chik-fil-A, we'd treat them to lunch; or if we wanted to go to a coffee shop, we'd buy them their favorite smoothie or drink.

Jill: Even though we'd outlined our standards for being together, it wasn't always easy to coordinate time for getting together. During one time when my family was out of town, it was especially hard, and I was reduced to tears. "I can't meet up with him because I don't have a chaperone!" I was really sad, but I prayed and trusted that if it was God's will, He would work it out. But it all worked out because one of Derick's coworkers was available to meet us for lunch.

Another time when we were having difficulty finding a chaperone so we could meet up when we were out and about, I tried to find a creative solution: "What if we could meet up real quick at a public place and have a chaperone observe us over FaceTime?" But when we thought about it, we knew that wasn't wise. Besides being unwise for us, it would also give the appearance of wrongdoing. And we wanted to live in a way that was above reproach. But somehow we figured it out and were able to meet up that evening. It was fun to see how God answered our prayers even in small ways. We also learned that making sure we had a chaperone wasn't just a matter of sticking to the rules; it was really a matter of having the right heart.

NEW from Derick and Jill . . .

Derick: I HAD HAD a couple of girlfriends before meeting Jill, and chaperoning was new to me. But just because I had handled relationships one way in the past didn't mean I couldn't do it differently going forward. The same is true for you. I wish I had done things differently in my previous relationships, but I want you to understand that God gives grace to the humble. As I try to submit every area of my life to God, He gives me the grace to live my life for Him. And when we make the effort to do that, God will bless our efforts.

Jill: You may be wondering how you might handle your relationships with guys going forward. You may have already had your first kiss; you may have even given away the physical side of yourself. But I want you to know that if you desire for your future relationships or a present relationship to be handled in a more careful way, God will help you follow through with your conviction. No matter how far you've gone, the past is behind you, and you can't change that. But you can change how you behave in relationships with guys in the future. None of us is perfect and none of us ever "arrives"; we're not going to be where we want to be this side of heaven. But we do want to continually become more like Christ. Jesus was perfect and He's our example. Being like Jesus should be our goal. Remember, Christianity is not about being perfect, but about being forgiven. The Bible says a righteous person will fall down seven times and will rise up seven times (Proverbs 24:16).

GUARDING YOUR HEART

WHEN WE COMMIT OUR life to God, we're saying, "Yes, God, I want You to guide me." We give God the position as "boss" and "ruler" of our lives, and we release the "steering wheel" to His control. But there may be times when we begin to fear that if certain things are left up to Him, they won't turn out the way we want them to. For instance, we may wonder, *What would happen if I truly gave God control over my love life?* And we may start to worry that He'll call us to be single till we're thirty! But when we hold something back, we're really taking control of the "steering wheel" again and trying to find our own path. This will only do us harm.

Shortly before Mom met Dad, she had a boyfriend who was a popular football player at her school. When she became a Christian at the age of fifteen and was so excited about the things of God, she tried to talk to this boyfriend about her newfound faith, but he didn't want to hear it. Mom struggled with the thought of breaking up with this guy—until she went to see the school counselor, who was also a Christian.

It wasn't like Mom had been resisting God altogether, but this one area—her boyfriend—was something she was hanging on to. She says that when she gave her life to God, she opened the door to her heart and said, "God, I want You to come in and take control." But as God began to convict her of different things in her life, it was as if she thought about her boyfriend and said, "I don't want to give that up!"

It was as though she built a little closet, put the boyfriend in there, and then said, "God, here's this area of my life that I'm willing to give up for You: music, movies, and clothing styles." But it felt as if God bypassed those things and went straight to that little closet and began to knock, asking, "Are you willing to give Me *this*?"

The counselor asked Mom, "Michelle, are you trusting Jesus to take you to heaven when you die?"

Mom responded, "Yes!"

"Then don't you think you can trust God with your love life?" he asked.

Mom said she'd never thought of it that way. She realized that God was more concerned with her future than she could ever be and that if she could trust Him for salvation, she could surely trust Him with the guy she would marry. So she prayed and said, "God, if this is not Your will, please make it easy for me to let go."

And God did. That next week they broke up, and just a few weeks later, God brought Dad into Mom's life.

The Bible tells us, "Keep thy heart with all diligence, for out of it are the issues of life" (Proverbs 4:23). Guarding our hearts must be important if the Bible says our very life depends on it!

NEW from Jessa . . .

WHEN YOUR HEART DRAWS close to a man emotionally, it is only natural that you desire to be close physically, too. This is not a bad desire—God designed us this way, but He has provided only one way for physical desires to be fulfilled without guilt, and that is through marriage. God has very clearly told us to confine sexual intimacy to marriage, and when we do, it is a beautiful thing! It's a wonderful thing!

We are often asked: *Do you really think it's wrong to kiss before marriage?* Let me say this up front: The Bible does not say, "Thou shalt not kiss before marriage." But 1 Corinthians 7:1 says, "It is good for a man not to touch a woman." Ben and I both felt like it was important not to stir up sensual desires before we said "I do," and so we made the decision not to kiss before marriage. We have heard someone say that if a couple cannot have physical self-control before marriage, then that can lead to a lack of trust in each other after marriage and to unnecessary guilt. Each person needs to ask himself or herself, "Is kissing before marriage wise?" The Bible says that there are some things that may be lawful, but they may also be very unhelpful. Some things may be "okay," but they may cause us to become even more desirous of premature physical intimacy. Embracing one another and being very close physically can stir up some serious desires that cannot be righteously fulfilled before marriage.

One other point is, when a couple has waited on the physical relationship until marriage, it sure makes you appreciate it after you get married. Many couples who decide not to wait, and even girls who give in to their boyfriend's pressure, often end up living together with no commitment to each other. A relationship built only on the physical will normally not last. When just living together, there is no lifelong commitment to staying together for better or for worse, or until death do you part. A lot of guys use girls for sex partners, without truly, unconditionally loving the girl; and as soon as a conflict arises, he moves on to the next girlfriend to fulfill his lustful desires. Ben desired to love me like Ephesians 5:25 says, "Christ loved the church, and gave himself for it." In a relationship, look how you can show love and cherish your future spouse, not what you can get out of the relationship. When both people love Jesus and give 110 percent to each other, this makes for a dynamic relationship!

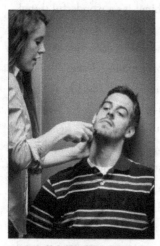

Derick and I (Jill) decided to circumvent the tradition of not seeing each other on the day of the wedding and instead spent as much time together as possible on this big day. We had devotions together, I gave him a trim on his facial hair, and we quickly got ready, then took our "first look" photos! I found that getting to be together on that big day relieved loads of stress that brides usually feel!

NEW from Jill . . .

I JUST WANT TO add one brief thought here. Before Derick and I began our courtship, I knew of him through my dad, who had frequent phone conversations with him as a prayer partner. So I had thought a little about Derick and had even prayed about a possible relationship. But I also prayed that God would not allow me to think seriously about any guys until it was His timing for me to begin a relationship with "the one."

SO HOW DO WE guard our hearts before marriage? We begin by taking every dream and desire to the Lord in prayer and believing and trusting that

His plan for our lives is best. His plan, carried out in His timing and His way, will bring us into the marriage He intends for us—*if* He intends marriage for us.

While we wait for God to bring the man He intends for us to marry into our lives, we strive to harness that desire for marriage and use and direct those energies toward impacting the world for Him. The way we serve God is by ministering to and serving others.

The Bible tells the stories of those who achieved great accomplishments for God during their youth. We can learn so much from them! For example, Daniel was taken captive as a young teen but counseled four kings and was made ruler of one of the largest empires of his time, all because he honored and served God in his youth.

God used a young woman named Esther to save the entire Jewish nation.

At age seventeen, Joseph was sold by his brothers into slavery, and yet God later used him powerfully to save Israel and Egypt from famine.

God is able to use you to do great things for Him, too. Devote yourself to serving God, and even though you are young, He can use you to impact the world for Him.

Visiting places like Honduras and sharing
the gospel with villagers is a ministry
opportunity our family greatly treasures.

INVOLVING OUR PARENTS IN
OUR LIFE-PARTNER DECISION

DURING THESE YEARS AS single adults, we want to prepare for the time when God brings the man He intends for us to marry into our lives. This includes studying the Bible to gain principles and standards that will be foundational in our future marriages. It is also important to seek counsel from the ones who love us most (our parents and siblings) and get their advice on any guy we think might be a potential mate. They will be able to examine the guy more objectively than we can because they want what is best for us and will be able to identify character deficiencies that we might overlook. As the wise saying goes, guys can see through guys like girls can see through girls.

NEW from Jill . . .

WHEN I CONFIDE IN my parents, they always guard what I say and keep it to themselves. This makes us feel safe when talking openly with them, and I have always appreciated that security. Knowing that I could trust my parents with my heart made it so much easier to share my concerns, worries, and struggles. And because I was used to sharing with them when I was younger, it made it easier for me to share with them while in my relationship with Derick.

If you don't have a good family network, don't depend on the advice of a peer or immature friend who is making bad decisions with their own life. Find a pastor's wife or a mature Christian woman you can be accountable to. It really helps to have someone to walk and talk through life with you. My parents know that each child is different and that each situation is different. They were able to see that Ben's and Jessa's personalities were different from mine and Derick's, so when they offered advice and counsel, it was individualized.

NEW from Ben . . .

MY DAD WAS THE one who put a fire under me. He encouraged me to take initiative and to get a job. And he did this long before I met Jessa. I worked with my dad replacing car windshields, so I learned a good work ethic. After I met Jessa, I talked to my dad about what I should do. I asked him what he thought and if I should court her. He gave me some good advice. He said, "Don't just wait around. If you think

While taking a walk together, we (Jessa & Ben) came across some heart-shaped leaves and decided to take a picture! This was shortly after we got engaged!

this is who God wants you to be with, take action." My mom was also very supportive—she always let me know she was there for me. My parents had courted as well, so they helped me to see that courting has the distinct purpose of helping us get to know someone. It is not just casual dating. Even though my parents hadn't always had a chaperone while they courted, they encouraged Jess and me to have one.

NEW from Derick . . .

MY PARENTS DATED FOR five years before they got married. They may not have called it courting, but they taught me not to pursue anyone I would not consider marrying. Growing up, I lived only about forty-five minutes from where Jill lived, but she and I had to go eight thousand miles across the world to meet each other. Here's how we met: While I was doing some humanitarian work in Nepal, Jill's dad was one of my prayer partners. We talked every couple of weeks to discuss how our work was going and what our current prayer needs were. As we talked, Jill's dad began to mention the work Jill was doing in her studies as a student midwife and her desire to someday use her skills overseas on the mission field. When I learned we had similar life goals, that caught my attention. The first time Jill and I spoke was over the phone in a brief conversation we had back in March 2013. I continued speaking with Jim Bob (Jill's dad) over the summer, but didn't speak with Jill again until August. However, during this time I prayed about Jill and asked God for direction in getting to know her better.

The answer to my prayer came in August 2013, just before I left Nepal for a two-week trip to Japan. During a conversation with Jim Bob, he mentioned that he thought Jill and I might get along well since we had similar personalities and direction in life. He gave me Jill's phone number, and Jill and I began texting, then emailing, then Skyping. Over the next few months, we became very grateful for modern technology, as we continued to get to know each other better. Most of our conversations were centered around our values and life goals.

At the end of November, Jill and her dad came to Nepal for a couple of weeks. I had no idea what to expect, but I was excited and prayed that God would give me clear direction during this time. By the end of the trip, I felt the Lord directing me to ask Jill to officially begin a courtship relationship. She agreed, and we continued getting to know one another. It would still be two months before I completed my two-year term and moved back home to Arkansas.

Upon my arrival home (January 2014), I was met by the whole Duggar clan—this was my first time to meet Jill's family in person. Over the next few months, I enjoyed spending time getting to know Jill and her family better. I was so thankful for the involvement of both our parents, as we walked this new time in our lives.

OFTENTIMES, WHEN A GIRL becomes emotionally attracted and attached to a guy, she begins to look at him through rose-colored glasses. But then once she's married, out comes the microscope! The problems were probably there from the beginning, but she couldn't see them because of her emotional attachment.

If a guy catches our eye or shows some interest in one of us and we think he might have some potential, we probably would ask Dad or one of our older brothers what they think of him and get their advice. If it becomes clear this interest is mutual and growing, the guy is directed to talk to our dad, who then is able to go over certain things with the guy and determine his character and goals in life. He may want to know things like . . .

- Is he a believer in Jesus? Does he know and love God?
- Does he have a vision for his life of doing great things for God?
- Is he free of all harmful addictions such as pornography, alcohol, drugs, immorality, etc.?
- Is he given to anger, lust, bitterness, greed, or envy?
- Is he wise with his finances?
- Does he love children? (The answer to this one is probably apparent as soon as he steps foot on Duggar property!)
- Is he a man of character, showing initiative, creativity, diligence, enthusiasm, and wisdom?
- Are both sets of parents giving their full and unreserved permission and blessing for their children to pursue this relationship?
- Does he have similar convictions and standards to ours? (How long has he had them? Some lifestyle choices are just opinions and flexible; others are nonnegotiable.)
- Has he been married or in a relationship before? (If he has made a marriage vow to another woman, he needs to keep that vow!)

- Is his passion in life for earthly money or for eternal riches and rewards?
- Does he accept me just the way I am?
- Could I say he loves God more than he loves me? Will he draw me closer to God?
- *Does he love me?*

If Mom and Dad agree that the young man has a heart for the Lord and a potential as a future spouse, then we will invite him to visit our family so we can get to know each other in our normal life (group) setting. And we'll also hope to visit him in his family setting as well.

If a young man comes to visit our family, he might just be invited to join in a game of Monopoly—one of our favorite games.

~

NEW from Derick . . .

JIM BOB ASKED ME questions like, "You're in this relationship now. How are you going to support your family?" He also asked broad questions that were important to address. He already knew me some as a prayer partner, but now that I might be courting his daughter, he wanted more information. He asked me about my previous relationships with girls and about how my mom felt about Jill and me courting. He asked me what my spiritual struggles were and how I was addressing them. Even though the conversations were a bit awkward at times, I appreciated his concern for Jill and for us as a couple.

NEW from Jill . . .

AS DERICK SAID, HE and my dad had a prayer-partner relationship for about a year and a half. My dad was impressed with Derick, and his confidence made me feel more secure about getting to know Derick better. My dad said we might have a lot in common, and suggested that we start texting. Whenever Derick and I started communicating, I asked even more questions than my dad did.

~

UNDERSTANDING HOW COURTSHIP DIFFERS FROM DATING

THERE ARE SOME VERY real and very purposeful differences between courtship and dating—and we believe the principles of courtship result in wise and safe choices.

1. Real-Life Settings

Getting to know the special young man we're interested in within a family setting is one of the biggest differences in dating and courtship. A danger of modern dating is that it is typically two young people, alone, enjoying an activity. Usually a guy invites a girl out to a nice restaurant or some fun place or event. They enjoy a carefree time without the responsibility of the normal tasks and pressures of life. For instance, if a guy invites you to have dinner at a restaurant, someone else makes your food exactly to your liking and then clears your dishes for you while the guy looks deep into your eyes and says whatever nice things he thinks you want to hear.

Now, all of us would surely enjoy a few romantic dinners later on, but first we want to get acquainted with our young man in a normal family setting, where we'll be watching to see how he treats our brothers and sisters. We want to see how he reacts to normal family events, such as Josie accidentally spilling her milk in his lap, Jackson unintentionally ruining his board game, or Joseph trouncing him in a basketball match. We need to know how he handles frequent interruptions such as Jennifer and Johannah racing through the room on scooters, intruding on his conversation. We want to see how he interacts with the other kids if we have to excuse ourselves momentarily to help Mom or Dad with something.

It's pretty easy for a young man to put on a show of good conduct during a romantic, one-on-one date. We want to know if he's willing to work hard and build a solid relationship amid real-life scenarios.

And here's another biggie: how a man treats his parents and siblings (as well as our own) shows us how he is likely to treat his own future family. You simply won't see that by spending time alone with him.

We saw a good example of how family interaction can reveal someone's character a few years ago when we were traveling out east and some friends invited us to their house for a big gathering. That afternoon, a young man and his younger sister joined a few of us in a game of volleyball. As we were playing, the guy's sister went for the ball, but she slipped in the sand court and instead of hitting it over the net she caused it to bounce out of bounds. The young man said some demeaning things to his little sister, and a while later he actually threw a ball at her, just being mean and frustrated.

All of us Duggar girls took note of how he treated his sister. And to be honest, we were shocked. Dad saw what happened, and he cautioned the young man, "If you treat your sister that way today, you may well treat your wife that way someday in the future."

The guy simply laughed off Dad's warning by joking, "Well, my wife will just have to learn to get out of my way."

The guy evidently didn't learn anything from what happened that day. But we sure did!

A "real-life" setting for our family might include our whole
family having an adventure in a speedboat.

2. Accountability

Another difference between dating and courtship is *accountability*. When you're alone with a guy in a dating situation, with no one else around to hold you accountable, it's easy to put yourself into physical and moral danger and give in to those emotions or sensual thoughts that promise pleasant, but only temporary, fulfillment. Please don't put yourself in this situation!

NEW from Jill . . .

DERICK AND I MADE a list of our standards for being together. Of course, we couldn't think of every situation we might be in, so as things came up, we would reevaluate. One day we were sledding, and we were riding on the same sled. After we thought about it, we decided that wasn't something we should do. We learned to err on the side of caution rather than putting ourselves into situations where we might be tempted.

NEW from Derick . . .

OUR CHAPERONES WEREN'T THE ones who set the standards of what we could and couldn't do. But we let them know the standards we had set for ourselves. We typed out our list in a Word document and showed it to them. We told them what we thought was okay to do and what we agreed we should not do. It was good to have another pair of eyes helping us consider how our behavior might appear to others. We had to be sure to have the right attitude toward our chaperones. If you have the mind-set that when your chaperone turns around, you can do something that's not in your guidelines, then it's time to check your heart. You've asked them to be there for you, and they want to help you out.

Our chaperones put in a lot of hours with us and we really appreciated it. Maybe they should get smart and start charging!

HERE ARE SOME CAUTIONS to think about before putting yourself in a situation where you are alone with a guy:

First, if a guy cannot control himself with you before he is married, how are you going to trust him around other women after you marry him?

Second, once you open the door to being alone and enter into a physical relationship before marriage (kissing, touching, physical intimacy), you are allowing your partner to unwrap a precious, special gift that God intended you to hold on to until your wedding day, and you're also creating a lot of guilt and distrust, and you won't be able to fully enjoy the pleasure of the sin because of all the guilt it brings.

Third, an analogy Dad uses is that, as young children, he told us not to go near or play in the street, not because he wanted to take away our fun, but because he didn't want us to get hit by one of the many semi-trucks that drive past our house. In the same way, God has created physical intimacy to be a wonderful wedding gift for pleasure and bonding and to procreate children, but if it is done prematurely or with multiple partners, the very thing that was created to bring joy can bring sexually transmitted diseases such as HIV, herpes, and human papillomavirus (HPV),

We (Jill & Derick) saved our first kiss for our wedding day, and it was well worth it!

which can cause infertility, cervical cancer, and a life sentence of pain and suffering.

HPV is just one of many sexually transmitted viruses, but it has recently become a notorious killer of women. According to the National Cancer Institute, "Virtually all cervical cancers are caused by HPV infections." The American Cancer Society estimates that 4,030 women will die from cervical cancer this year. STDs like HPV also carry a high risk of being passed on to loved ones, including the woman's husband or her children.

What could be worse than having to tell your potential future husband that not only did you not wait but that you also have a severely painful STD that he will likely get if he marries you?

Physical intimacy in marriage is pure, wholesome, and beautiful. Outside of marriage, it spreads disease, death, and destruction. Just as Dad gave us kids boundaries to protect us from playing in the street, God gives boundaries as well. He wants to protect us from these hazards, and He will give us an abundant marriage if we do things in the order and timing He prescribes.

~~~

NEW from Jessa . . .

SOMETIMES WHEN GIRLS ARE struggling with purity, they say, "But I want to be close to him! I want to be affectionate and show him how much I love him!" Okay, so this just means you are normal. When a girl is attracted to a guy, naturally she wants to be close to him. You may worry that if you don't express your love physically, he may think you don't really love him. But as we said earlier in the book, *true love waits*. It waits to be expressed within the boundaries of marriage—and there only. And maybe you are feeling pressured by your boyfriend. If this is the case, he is not demonstrating true love for you.

Real love helps the one we love to grow closer to Jesus Christ. True love speaks through your actions and says, "I want you to love Jesus more than you love me. I would never want you to stumble into sin as a result of me. Your relationship with God is more important to me than your relationship with me." When we love *selfishly*, we seek to draw the other person only to ourselves. *Selfish* love seeks gratification now, no matter what God says. So ask yourself, "Is my heart's desire to draw my boyfriend only closer to me, or is my goal to point him to a closer relationship with Jesus?" "Do my actions honor God or am I displeasing Him?"

FOURTH, A BABY IS a blessing no matter how it is conceived, but it is a lot more difficult to raise a child as a single mom. A huge percentage of the guys who have gotten a girl pregnant do not take responsibility for the child or want to have anything to do with the girl once she is pregnant.

If a guy is pressuring you to have a physical relationship with him and telling you, "If you loved me you would do this," tell him if he truly loves you he will wait until your wedding day and not steal your purity.

If you have already crossed that line, ask God to forgive you and then recommit yourself to staying pure from this point on until you get married. Several women in the Bible made major moral mistakes in their pasts, but they repented (that means changed their ways) and God used them in a mighty way in the future. Many times, Jesus said those who have been forgiven much love God and others in a deeper way because they are so thankful for all the forgiveness they have received.

If you are already pregnant, scared, and don't know what to do, don't allow anyone to talk you into taking the life of your child. Your baby is not a blob of tissue! Have you ever seen an ultrasound? About the time you realize you missed your cycle and wonder if you're pregnant, your baby's heart has already started beating, its eye and hair color are already determined, and its brain has already formed. It's a baby from the time it is conceived.

Even though this is happening out of God's designed order, He loves you both and will forgive you. Look online for a Christian crisis pregnancy center in your area, and the staff and volunteers there will assist you in this new phase of life. Don't ever consider getting an abortion, with a surgical procedure or with the abortion pill.

Abortion might seem like a quick fix to a big problem, but we personally know several women who have done this, and they have said they regret ending the life of their baby; it haunts them every day. You cannot get unpregnant. If you are pregnant, take responsibility and take care of yourself and your baby, and God will take care of you.

3. Pre-Courtship

Another difference between dating and courtship is that dating may or may not have marriage as its goal. Often it's just for fun, and for many young people, dating and physical intimacy go hand in hand. Modern-day dating tends to revolve around a self-centered relationship that is all about *me*: what makes *me* feel good and who makes *me* happy, satisfied, and "complete"—if only for a few moments. You may feel good or wanted for a little while, but pursuing these kinds of careless relationships will leave you feeling emotionally and spiritually empty in the end.

In contrast, we believe that the better alternative to casual dating is a pre-courtship (no-commitment) time period. In pre-courtship, if a guy and gal thinks they have some interest in each other, they can get to know each other in a group setting through activities before courtship is ever considered.

4. *Official Courtship*

Once they get to know each other and the guy and girl and both sets of parents are agreed that this appears to be God's will, the couple can move into an official courtship, which is a commitment period and a time for the guy to begin winning the girl's heart, with a potential end goal of a short engagement to plan a wedding, then marriage.

Courtship is a serious commitment and should only be carried out by those for whom marriage is a realistic possibility. Much care needs to go into making sure that this is the man you desire to spend the rest of your life with.

NEW from Jessa . . .

THE DAY BEN AND I started courting, we began our tradition of calling each other on the phone every night! These were such special times. We would talk about everything from how our day went, to what we had been learning from our Bible reading, and then just anything else that we wanted to talk about. These calls were not "chaperoned." They were private—just between the two of us. This was a time for us to talk heart-to-heart and get to know each other even better. We would try to limit our phone time to an hour, but many times the conversation was so rich and deep that we'd have to go into overtime! We always ended our phone time by praying together.

5. *A Time of Observation*

NEW from Jill and Jessa . . .

SINCE WE WROTE THE original edition of this book, two of us have been through courtship and gotten married—and yes, we're talking about us—Jill and Jessa! After much prayer, counsel, and consideration, we each felt that it was God's will and God's timing to get married. Our parents had taught us that when Mr. Right came along, we would have a peace in our hearts and that God would confirm our choice through our parents. But until that happened, we chose to be content in the phase of our lives when we were single and tried to live every *single* day for the Lord. As you are waiting for God's leading, we encourage you to keep your eyes focused on Him and to trust His timing.

DAD HAS CAUTIONED US girls not to give a hesitant yes to the first guy who comes along, out of fear that we may never get another guy. At the same time, we know we shouldn't turn a guy away just because we have our sights set on someone else. Dad has encouraged us to not only evaluate a man's character but also compare his personality type with ours and con-

Ben with his groomsmen.

sider other things to see if we would truly be compatible.

So, in the meantime, we girls see this time not as a time to eagerly *search* for that perfect soul mate—but as a time to *observe* the characteristics in the young men we interact with.

It's natural for every girl and boy, somewhere around the age of twelve, to begin noticing each other as more than just childhood playmates and start thinking more along the lines of searching for their future soul mate.

If a girl isn't careful, she can gain an emotional attachment to a guy prematurely during this phase, and before either of them is ready for marriage, she will already be dreaming of his last name with her first, and what a cute couple they would make, and engagement rings, and wedding colors, and on and on.

So instead of getting wrapped up in the *search*, we want to share some of the things we've been taught to *observe*.

You can learn so much about a guy through simply observing his interactions with others—whether he respects his parents, how he treats his siblings, who his close friends are. And by observing his personal conduct—how he chooses to spend his time, what things he esteems, what things he laughs at, how he takes losses, if he is setting worthwhile goals or is just aimlessly wandering through life.

NEW from Jessa . . .

A LOT OF GUYS try to put on a good show for their girl. So when I first hung out with Ben's family, I was interested in what his siblings would say about him, and they all spoke very highly of him. Ben's brothers said he was the best big brother in the whole world. They said he was always there for them, that he was compassionate, and that if they'd had a hard day, he was the one they wanted to talk to. I thought this was the response I would get from his siblings, but it was very encouraging to hear it firsthand.

WE CAN ALSO LEARN a lot about a guy through wholesome communication and group interaction. Not on the flirtatious junior high level that shouts *I like you* but through meaningful conversations about history, politics, theology, and such. When we approach our friendships with guys on a less personal, more businesslike level, we're able to spot things we would totally miss if we had already drowned out our reasoning in a sea of emotional attachment.

IDENTIFYING CHARACTER QUALITIES
WE HOPE FOR IN A FUTURE HUSBAND

WE'RE NOT SAYING THE goal is to find a perfect person. As far as we know, no such person exists. We all make mistakes and need God's forgiveness, and so will the young man God brings to you. On the other hand, it's unlikely that an angry, self-centered man who is lazy and a poor money manager will suddenly evolve into Husband and Dad of the Century.

We're also not saying he has to be the best-looking hunk of human flesh ever created. Sure, we all look at outward appearances and at first may be attracted to an individual based on his looks. But God urges us to see what He sees: the condition of the heart. Galatians 5:22 gives a great list of qualities to look for in a potential spouse. If a guy you are considering is not growing in peace, joy, patience, kindness, goodness, faithfulness, gentleness, and self-control, he's just not a good marriage prospect, no matter how handsome or successful he seems! Remember, you're considering not only what kind of husband you will have but also what kind of father your children will have.

NEW from Jill . . .

I HAVE TO ADMIT, I was nervous at the beginning of our relationship. I later told Derick that asking him all those questions at the beginning of our relationship was kind of like throwing up—you hate doing it, but you feel much better afterward. I know that sounds gross, but with throwing up, you know you'll feel better after, but the throwing up part is awful!"

To help me identify a possible future husband, I used a list of Courtship Questions a friend had shared with me. Before our first Skype call, I also spent two hours going over my journal from the past few years—reviewing the character qualities I had listed for someone I might marry. So in addition to the Courtship Questionnaire and my notes from my journal, we also told each other stories about our lives. My thinking was that I wanted to ask as many questions and get to the heart of deeper matters early on in the relationship, so I would reduce the possibility of either of us getting hurt. Don't get me wrong, I know not every relationship ends in marriage, but I didn't want this relationship to go on for six months and then, when I'd finally build up enough courage to ask the tougher questions, find out we didn't agree and would need to end things there. I wanted to get all the big stuff out. That first Skype call was five and a half hours!

My mom used to tell me that you'll know a lot about a guy by the way he spends his free time, so I asked Derick, "What do you enjoy doing?" And since Derick's dad had passed away, I asked him, "What is the biggest character quality your dad taught you?" And I asked

For our honeymoon, we stayed at the outer banks of North Carolina. Our rental home was right on the beach! Here we are visiting Cape Hatteras.

him how his dad treated his mom. I considered that however he saw his parents treating each other was how he'd treat his wife (or maybe veer away from it). I asked him, "What do you believe about drinking?" and many other questions. I really grilled Derick in the beginning of our relationship.

Our first Skype call was really good, and I was encouraged. But I had to remind myself that even if I went through my lists and asked the tough questions and checked all my boxes—still not every relationship ends in marriage. I had to remember that God can take relationships that don't end in marriage and use them to grow us into better people. I had to ask myself, *Is my heart already tied to him so much that it would be hard to break it off?*

While we were getting to know each other, my dad also sent Derick a questionnaire to fill out and had him go through different seminars and things that had influenced him.

A Godly Man, like Our Dad

What all of us Duggar girls hope for is a husband like our dad. (But we know that's asking a lot!) Dad has demonstrated a selfless attitude over the years and has given of himself in so many ways, modeling to us the heart of a true servant, and that's certainly something we would desire in a future husband.

At one time during their early married years, Dad worked multiple jobs to keep things afloat and to maintain his and Mom's resolve that she would stay home with us kids. And even at the end of a long workday, he has always made time to play with his kids, no matter how tired or exhausted he may be.

He especially loves to do little extras for Mom and even us girls. On occasion he has taken us out for special father-daughter dates, and often when he's getting something like flowers or a coffee for Mom, he'll get something for us, too. Plus, while Dad makes the boys save up and buy a car of their own, it has been his goal to provide his girls with vehicles to drive, just as an extra expression of a dad's love and care for his girls.

Dad would be the first to tell you that God has "grown him" a lot over the years. Growing up, Dad didn't have much of a father figure himself. But when he was about ten years old, he was reading through the book of James and came across the verse that says, "If any man lack wisdom, let him ask of God, which giveth to all men liberally and upbraideth not, and it shall be given him."

Dad stopped right then and asked God for wisdom. He desired to be a spiritual leader for his own family one day. God heard his prayer and gave him wisdom and guidance. When he and Mom were married at a young age, God guided him through His Word, the Bible, and also allowed him to learn through the good examples of some other men at church.

Today, Dad is not a perfect man, but he is a humble man, and he's not afraid to admit his mistakes and ask forgiveness if he messes up. Dad is a man of character. He treats Mom with love and respect, he provides for our family, and he supports Mom fully in running our home. He praises her efforts, and he never belittles her, makes fun of her, or uses her as a negative example for anything.

Dad and Jessa enjoy a special treat together.

He also makes his family a priority. Dad doesn't own a bass boat, doesn't take weeklong hunting trips with his buddies, and doesn't spend Saturday mornings on the golf course with his men friends. He says his children are his hobby, and he obviously loves being with us. He is our family's spiritual leader—and also its number-one cheerleader. We just hope our children are as blessed by their father as we are by ours!

That would mean we desire the man we marry to be honest, hardworking, generous, and ministry-focused. It doesn't mean we have our hearts set on marrying a pastor. A man doesn't have to be a pastor or in full-time ministry, because as Christians, we are to be a light wherever God places us. In our eyes, there is no difference between full-time ministry and being a Christian mechanic or a Christian doctor or a Christian politician. We need more men who are willing to proclaim Christ in the workplace and realize that there is no such thing as an off-duty Christian. We just pray that, whatever work our future husband does, he uses it as a ministry for God.

~~~

NEW from Jill . . .

BEFORE I KNEW DERICK, he and some fellow carolers from his church had stopped by our house to sing. Neither of us remembers each other from this encounter, but I do have a vague memory of the group coming to our home. It was soon after this that Derick reached out to my dad and asked if he would be a prayer partner while he was in Nepal. It was through this prayer relationship that my dad first got to know Derick—and Dad was very impressed with his godly character. So Dad started telling me about Derick and also told Derick about me! I actually listened in on a few phone conversations with my dad without Derick knowing.

After I kept hearing such good things about this guy, I decided I'd look him up on my own, so I Googled him and got a little glimpse from his social media outlets. I thought it was really neat that we had similar life goals.

NEW from Jessa . . .

I HAVE GREAT ADMIRATION and respect for my dad, and now being in a relationship with my husband, I love and admire him even more! I remember the many conversations Ben and I had when he would come up to visit my family's church. We had him over to our house many a Sunday afternoon, and we could sit around for hours and talk about things from the Scriptures. He wasn't just a "Sunday Christian." I could tell that this man really read and studied his Bible and that he loved the Lord with all of his heart. We developed a friendship that deepened with the passing months. The more I got to know about him, the more I admired him.

Ben and I asked each other so many questions about one another's beliefs on a variety of topics, and we carried on conversations about things we were learning from our individual Bible studies. I was inspired by Ben's love for God and his desire to read the Word. I was touched by his heart of compassion for the hurting and his desire to bring hope to the hopeless. When I read the gospel tracts that he had written and heard stories of how he would reach out to the lost, I thought to myself, *How many young people out there are like this?* The more I found out about this man, the more I admired and was drawn to him.

This picture was taken in Venice, Italy, during our
(Jessa & Ben's) ten-day European honeymoon!

A Gentle Spirit

We've already mentioned anger as a red flag to avoid at all costs. But it's such a destructive character flaw that we want to talk about it a little more before we move on. Our goal is to find a man who has a gentle, kind spirit—not one who regularly loses his temper and spews out anger. I (Jana) mentioned in an earlier chapter how sad it was for me to hear girl after girl during Journey to the Heart retreats say that her dad's anger had caused what seemed to be irreparable harm and hurt within her family.

The truth is that all of us must learn to deal with our own emotions and feelings when something doesn't go the way we hoped. The Bible says we should all strive to be "swift to hear, slow to speak, slow to wrath" (James 1:19). Often, the way a person responds to a situation is even worse than the situation itself. We recall an incident that happened years ago, ironically during fellowship time after church. Every week, it is our custom to share a meal together after the service and spend time, sometimes several hours, talking and sharing fellowship with other families in the church.

During the fellowship time one hot Sunday afternoon, Jill thought it would be fun for all the kids to have a water balloon fight. She made sure Dad was okay with the plan and then recruited younger brother James and a couple other siblings to help her fill several dozen balloons with water.

Finally they carried the buckets of balloons outside, and soon the water bombs began to fly. The kids had a great time: lots of shrieks and running and throwing with water splattering in all directions.

When a dad of a visiting family heard the noise and saw his children were getting wet, he came outside and exploded in rage, "Who said you could do that?"

Everyone froze as he continued to shout in anger.

Even though she was a rather confident sixteen-year-old at the time, Jill hid. His boiling anger frightened her. It frightened *all* the kids.

She later apologized to the family, and so did Dad, but the angry outburst made an impression.

Another memorable incident came about while we were on an outing to enjoy one of the Duggars' favorite sports: broomball. It's an offshoot of ice hockey but is played in tennis shoes instead of skates, and the goal is to get a ball into the net with something similar to a hockey stick. That means those lacking traditional hockey skills are welcome to play.

For several years we used to play broomball as a family at the local ice rink, which sets aside certain times for the game. Those sessions taught us that sports can reveal a lot about a person's character, including his or her temper. Being competitive is great, but many times we saw fits of anger from some of those competing. One night a young man, furious after losing, threw his broomball stick, smashing it against the wall so that pieces flew in all directions. And the stick wasn't even his!

We want to know right from the beginning if the young man we're interested in has a problem controlling his temper because if he does, that's something he needs to seriously work on before he even thinks of setting his sights on marriage.

~

NEW from Jessa . . .

WHEN BEN AND I were courting, one thing I really appreciated was his humility and gentle spirit. If he did something to hurt my feelings or took something the wrong way, he was quick to apologize. He'd say, "I'm sorry," and it was a sincere apology. That made me feel really loved. And Ben has never belittled my emotions, and he doesn't blow them off. I saw that when we were courting, and now that we're married, I continue to see that he's a sweetheart through and through. Who he was then is who he is now.

~

JUST AS IT'S HELPFUL to us to see how a guy reacts when one of our young siblings spills a cup of chocolate milk on his new shirt, it's also helpful to see how he responds in other situations, including sports. Is he angry or gracious in defeat? Does he fume for hours or congratulate the winner, put the loss behind him, and move on? Equally important is how he handles winning. Does he gloat and boast? Or does he shake hands with his opponent and offer encouragement?

Questions like these are more reasons why we believe in family visits and a variety of family activities during courtship rather than one-on-one dates. Don't get us wrong. There's a time and place for a romantic dinner date, and some good communication can be enjoyed in that setting. But a man's character may be more apparent by observing him in everyday situations and interactions.

Chivalry

It warms our hearts when we're around young men, including our brothers, who are courteous and quick to practice the fine old art of gentlemanly chivalry. Some women these days think that allowing men to help them with anything makes them appear weak, and they refuse to take a man's hand to help them down a step or object to a man's offer to help them carry a heavy load. However, a gentleman's courtesy is not about women being weak or strong; it's about men needing to be men. Gentlemanly behavior is cultivated as they learn to serve others and treat ladies as ladies. We encourage these efforts in our family— one reason being we know that somewhere out there, some good Christian girls are praying for the young man God intends as their future husband: a godly, courteous, thoughtful young man who might just turn out to be one of our brothers!

Every day, Dad seeks to model genuine chivalry for all of us. To the boys, it's an example of what they desire to become, and to us girls it's the mark of a gentleman and something we desire to see in our own spouse one day. Dad has always been sensitive and caring toward us kids, but he especially looks out for his girls. He made it known early on that the boys were to treat us girls with respect, and while we all enjoyed climbing trees or playing sports together, Dad would remind the boys we were not the chums who should receive a hard knuckle on the shoulder or a serious whack over the head during a friendly sibling pillow fight.

Dad always wants to demonstrate this kind of gentlemanly behavior for all of us, especially the boys, but sometimes he forgets. He asked us to help him with reminders when needed. Years ago, he was working on honoring Mom in several specific ways, including remembering to open the car door for her. He had always done this during the earlier years of marriage, but recently, since we'd outgrown our fifteen-passenger van and had to transport everyone in two separate cars, it hadn't been happening as frequently.

Mom agreed to help him remember to do this by waiting and giving him the opportunity to come around to her side of the car. One afternoon they headed to the local paint store to pick out paint for one of our rental houses, and just as Dad got out of the car he got a phone call. Distracted by the call, he proceeded on toward the store and was almost to the door, continuing his phone call, when Mom, still waiting in the car, leaned over and gently tapped the horn.

Dad turned around, puzzled, and spotted Mom, laughing and waving from the front seat of the car. Dad realized he had forgotten to open the car door for her and came running to get her. We kids laughed so hard that night as they recounted the entire event to us.

Apparently the horn-honking worked. Now Dad almost never forgets to the open the car door for Mom or any of us girls—but these

In all our travels, Dad especially looks out for his girls—making sure we are taken care of. Here we are in Nashville at the home of the Grand Ole Opry.

days our brothers often beat him to it! They are all striving to become courteous and thoughtful young men. When we were all at a restaurant recently, it was pouring down rain and Jedidiah jumped on his opportunity. He grabbed the only umbrella in the bus and, in groups of two, began escorting his mom and sisters inside. We didn't take this for granted. We praised his efforts and told him, "Jedidiah, you're such a gentleman. Thank you," and he beamed at the compliment.

The other day when we were all outside enjoying a vigorous game of volleyball, Justin disappeared inside and then came out carefully carrying a tray loaded with cups of ice water. "Care for a glass of water, ladies?" It sure hit the spot, and we thanked Justin profusely for his thoughtfulness.

James must have been listening, because a few days later, he did the same thing, bringing everyone water when we were all outside on a hot summer day.

Members of the TLC film crew, who have become like older brothers to us, have also encouraged us to marry a gentleman. When producer Sean took us girls to coffee awhile ago, he opened the door for us and said, "Chivalry isn't dead! Let me tell you something, gals: don't even consider marrying a guy who won't open the door for you."

Now, if you came to the Duggar household today, you would probably find some elbows on the dinner table and maybe even a boy who forgot to wash the dirt from behind his ears. But the goal in our household is for guys to treat gals with the upmost respect and honor by giving up their chair, opening doors, and looking for ways to put women and children first. Respect means a lot in our family, and courtesy counts.

Making a List

As we older Duggar girls (and boys) have entered this chapter of our lives, Dad has encouraged us to write out a list of things we desire in a future spouse. And no, this isn't a place to write down wishes for "tall, dark, and handsome," but to focus on character, personal standards, and other qualities. We already mentioned that some of the nonnegotiables are that he must be a Christian, and he must love Jesus as much as we do. He should have a love for children because the Bible says repeatedly that children are a blessing from God, a reward from Him.

In addition to being "slow to wrath," he needs to be a good steward of his money with a goal of living debt-free within his finances. And then there are the other character qualities we desire in a spouse, including gentleness, deference, and gratefulness.

~~~

NEW from Jessa . . .

OUR PARENTS HAVE TAUGHT us to look at a person's character even more than their personality. Things like: Is he looking for ways to give to others, not seeking anything in return, or is he a selfish man, always demanding his own way and seeking to make himself comfortable? Is he gentle or is he harsh? Is he compassionate and caring? Does he build people up with his words, or does he mock, scorn, and put others down? Will he admit when he has done something wrong and ask forgiveness, or is he stubborn and too proud to admit his faults?

As you're observing a potential husband, don't only look at the way he treats you. How does he treat his family? How is he around his friends? These are the things you need to know and observe about a man. A boyfriend with bad character today will not suddenly evolve into Husband of the Year tomorrow.

NEW from Jill . . .

AS I OBSERVED DERICK, I'd ask him what his opinion was on specific topics. If he didn't have an opinion one way or another about something, he wouldn't make something up just to look like he had an answer. Derick was genuine about saying, "I'm not sure what I think on that, but I'd like to study that and learn more." He definitely has a learning spirit, and that impressed me. He is not proud, and he's very gentle, and he's a perfect balance for me. God has provided above and beyond for me the things I had been praying about for a long time.

WHILE THIS LIST SERVES as a guide in our evaluation of a suitor, the reason for writing it up is *not* so that we can constantly be comparing it to every guy we meet, hoping the "glass slipper" will fit and he'll be our Prince-to-be! Dad has encouraged us to write out these lists so we can turn them around and use them to examine our own lives, asking ourselves, *Am I slow to anger? Am I wise with my finances? Am I striving to display these character qualities in my own life?* Everything we ask of others we must first demand of ourselves.

It has been interesting to see that the things that bug us the most about others' lives are often issues we struggle with ourselves to some degree. For instance, if we are extremely sensitive to someone else's arrogance, we should search our own hearts for an attitude of pride, whether it is in our achievements or in our voicing our strong opinions when it's not our place to do so.

Dad has reminded us that as Christian young ladies, it's vitally important that we always remember we have been adopted into the family of God, and our heavenly Father is the King of kings. It's also crucial for Christian gals to understand that we cannot conform our patterns to a thoughtless lifestyle and still expect to *somehow* marry

"I Do" and "I'm Due"! Jessa and I experienced a lot of exciting changes in one year!

a godly prince. We need to always keep in mind that if we desire to marry a godly man, then we must strive to become the kind of godly girl a godly man will be attracted to. God desires to see us grow in character and live by His principles, and for us to have a strong relationship with *Him*—which is the best foundation and preparation any of us can make for a future marriage relationship.

UNDERSTANDING WHAT CHRISTIAN GUYS LOOK FOR IN A FUTURE WIFE

SO FAR IN THIS chapter, we've talked about what we girls are looking for in a future husband. As we were pulling together information for this book, we thought it would also be interesting to ask some of our guy friends what they are looking for in a future wife. So we sent out a little survey, asking fifteen of them to answer a few questions. Obviously, this was a small and totally unscientific survey, and it went to our friends, many of whom share our Christian beliefs. They range in age from sixteen to twenty-nine, and their professions range from farming and construction to politics and graphic design. One is an attorney. Another is a Marine Corps officer.

All of them said they notice how a girl gets along with her parents and siblings.

Some said they watch her attitude in responding to her mom and dad.

When we asked the guys to describe, in one word, the most important character quality a Christian girl can have, we got these answers: integrity, purity, respectfulness, virtue, charity, and faith.

One guy said the most important character quality is "that she's *genuine.* Someone who's real in her love for people and in her compassion for others. Real in her heart for God and understanding of her own shortcomings."

Most of them said the first thing they notice about a girl is something related to her physical appearance: most surveyed said they like girls to have longer hair, they like girls who smile, and they appreciate when a girl is modest.

We asked the guys to name some things they're looking for in a girl. Here are some of their answers:

- Outgoing personality, not stuck-up, genuine love and loyalty toward her family, a girl who loves the Lord as much as I do and has a desire to share her faith.
- A girl who has a hunger and thirst after righteousness, one who is sensitive to the Holy Spirit.
- A girl who deeply cares about her faith (hearing and obeying the voice of God and fulfilling His purpose and calling for her life).
- Purity, ministry focus, compassionate spirit.
- A godly girl who honors her parents and who esteems motherhood.
- Is she sensitive to God's Spirit? Is she serving the Lord in her single years? Does she dress modestly?
- Good communication skills, common sense, love for Jesus.
- Always seeking God and not a relationship. If she gives her heart to God then God will give her heart to the right guy. Does not seek attention from guys by being flirtatious.
- A sweet, compassionate girl who exhibits genuine kindness leaves a deep impression on me. . . . An equally important quality is faithfulness. It's much harder to determine, but it's probably the final determining factor for me. I need someone to faithfully serve God alongside me, faithfully

hold me accountable, and someone to faithfully help me
grow deeper spiritually.

- A godly girl (reading the Bible, getting to know God deeper
  each day, and involved in some sort of ministry—preferably
  music ministry). I like it when I see a girl having a servant's
  heart and respecting her parents.
- A girl who demonstrates her love for God by honoring
  her parents, by treating her siblings like they are her best
  friends, and by being humble.
- Does she have a growing love for God, and are we on a
  similar path to knowing Him? Does her love of God form
  her character, values, and virtues? Can we help each other
  grow in the Lord?
- A godly, spiritually solid girl who has a good relationship
  with parents and a ministry mind-set!
- Does she have the character qualities of a Proverbs 31 woman?

NEW from Ben . . .

I USED TO WATCH Jessa and her family on TV when I would go to my
aunt's house to get my hair cut. At first I was struck by Jessa's magnifi-
cent beauty. But I really wanted to know what kind of a person she was.
On the show, I noticed that she was very articulate and seemed to have
a lot of wisdom. I saw one episode where she was leading a talk to some
girls about relationships with guys. Not only was the content of her talk
solid, but I was impressed with how good she was with words.

In another episode, I took note of her diligence, initiative, and responsibility as she helped out overseeing her siblings' computer-based
home education. When her mom was busy with baby Josie, Jessa
stepped up to the plate and helped her siblings with their schoolwork.
That's a big task in a family with nineteen kids!

I saw other qualities in her that I really admired, but I knew I needed to get to know her in person before I made the decision to seriously pursue her.

Once we met, I witnessed first-hand that she was very caring to her mother and helpful with her younger siblings. I had a few conversations with her and quickly realized that she liked to read and learn and that she had a considerable amount of knowledge on subjects I was interested in, such as theology, the family, church, education, etc. She seemed hungry to learn, and I perceived that she was a motivated individual.

Newlyweds!

For me, the most important thing I needed to know was whether she had a strong relationship with God. All the other virtues I saw in her were wonderful, but I wanted to know if she recognized the much greater importance of her relationship with God and how she was pursuing that. As I got to know her, I saw her passion for God and her devotion and loyalty to Him. She placed a great deal of importance on getting to know God better and reading and memorizing the Bible. As I saw this evidence of God's work in Jessa's heart and life, I knew that I could move forward and pursue a deeper relationship with her, if I had her parents' blessing.

As I got to know Jessa even more, I saw her maturity and her grasp of what was really important in life. She shared my love of studying the Bible and wanted to know what I believed. Seeing her in real-life situations, I learned that she wasn't putting on an act. She was the real deal.

Jessa is a go-getter. She's on a mission, and she knows how to get things done. She shows determination and leadership. One example of Jessa's diligence and work ethic had do to with our wedding gifts. I was thinking, *We'll send thank-you notes a few at a time,* but she got it all done in one day. Jessa is not a lazy woman! Not long ago, she and Jana painted their parents' room while they were away from home. Jessa was determined to get it done before they returned—and they did!

Some people place an exorbitant amount of emphasis on personality and whether their personalities complement each other. I was never set on a certain personality type. I didn't say, "I need a bold, outgoing girl." Or "I would go best with a sensitive, feeling, contemplative type of girl." My perspective was that if I got to know a girl, I was attracted to her, and, most important, she was a woman of God, then these things were far more important than personality compatibility from the world's perspective. Having the perfect personality match is overrated. Just say, for example, that my personality did clash with that of my wife. What a great opportunity to learn patience and to work through conflict by God's grace! In the end, with God's help, it would turn me into a more patient, less narrow person, who could get along well with any personality type.

NEW from Derick . . .

JILL AND I SPENT a lot of time together when she came to Nepal with her dad. I was able to see her interaction with other people. My goal and vision is to go into the mission field someday, so seeing her compassion for other people, her love, her service, and how sweet she is meant a lot to me. I also compared her to the Proverbs 31 woman and was so impressed with the qualities I saw. Jill was not just waiting for a guy to come along, but was complete in her relationship with God and was actively serving Him—and she still is.

Jessa with her bridesmaids.

NOW THAT WE'RE MARRIED

NEW from Jill and Jessa . . .

NOW THAT THE TWO of us have gone through courtship, engagement, and marriage, we wanted to share with you some of the things we experienced and learned about being engaged and now being married.

NEW from Jessa . . .

REMEMBER THAT THE SEASON of being single will not last forever. Once you and the young man you care about know for sure that you are meant for each other, for goodness sake, get married! I think it is very unwise to enter into a relationship if you cannot realistically marry within a year or two. If you do, you set yourself up for all kinds of temptations. If you think you can drag a premarital, romantic relationship out for years and years and still maintain absolute moral purity between the both of you, then you really need to rethink. Maybe it would be possible if you lived on opposite sides of the globe, but it's usually very unwise to put yourself in that kind of situation. Better to hold off getting emotionally attached to someone if you are not ready to be married. The closer two hearts grow, the stronger your soul ties become, and the more susceptible you will be to doing something you never thought you would do before you were married.

During the first couple of months of our marriage, Ben was still working on finishing up his college studies. Even during our honeymoon, he was studying for finals online and taking exams. But this is something we had talked about. We didn't think it was wise to wait when we knew we were getting married, because that could increase our temptation. This is how our timeline worked for us: We knew each other through church for about five months. Then we courted for eleven months, and were engaged for two and a half months. So once we were engaged, we really stepped up the tempo, so our wedding wouldn't be far off. During our first months of marriage, Ben was juggling a full-time job, full-time studies, and being a full-time husband; but by God's grace, it all worked out. And now Ben is praying about signing up for seminary! I'm blessed to be married to such a diligent, hardworking man. Our time together has been wonderful. I wouldn't trade these past few months for anything!

NEW from Ben . . .

I WANT TO ECHO what Jessa said. If you're trying to save yourself for marriage and stay pure until married, then it's important to not put yourself in a situation where that's difficult. Don't waste any time in getting married. Get to that point. Don't put it off.

NEW from Jill and Derick . . .

WE THOUGHT WE'D SHARE with you our list of guidelines during engagement, so you can see how it worked for us:

DO

- Say "I Love you!"
- Hold hands/arms
- Have heart-to-heart talks, including struggles
- Always have a chaperone within line of sight (Justin's age: eleven years old and up)
- Talk about the future
- Pray and talk in the morning (for a shorter time) and evening (longer)
- Share side hugs when coming and going (less than twenty seconds)
- Place head on shoulder or head on head
- Open car door
- Pull out chair
- Look into each other's eyes
- Encourage and edify each other in the Lord
- Study together
- Listen to sermon messages together
- Skype, FaceTime, and phone alone
- Then once you know this is God's will, with all parents on board, plan wedding (and get married quickly!!!)

DON'T

- Place arm on back of the other's chair

- Share frontal hugs
- Kiss
- Go in each other's bedroom (or sit on a bed alone together)
- Sled on same sled

OUT OF GRATITUDE FOR our siblings and friends giving of their time to chaperone us, we would try to do something nice for them in return! Here is a list of some of their preferred chaperone treats:

- James—Skittles
- Jason—GoGo applesauce
- Joy—Chik-fil-A
- Justin—Skittles
- Rachel—Acambaro tacos, chips, and salsa
- Jana—chips and salsa
- Venessa—chips and queso
- Jed—Daniel Boone and Sgt. York movies
- Noah—Skittles
- Abigail—Nerds and Skittles
- Elizabeth—Chik-fil-A

NEW from Jill . . .

SOMETIMES PEOPLE ASK ME if all the waiting and the being chaperoned and being so careful in our relationship was worth it. And I always say, "Absolutely yes!" But please know that we had the same emotions that anyone else would have. We're all human. It wasn't always easy, but by God's grace we stuck to our convictions. We would often pray, "Lord, please help us stay true to the standards we've set," because it was hard! But the boundaries we set before marriage and the joy of being together in marriage is all worth it.

Before I was married, I was always accountable to someone—

usually my parents. And that honest relationship gave me a pattern for how to talk openly and honestly about things. So when Derick and I got married, it wasn't so difficult to transfer that kind of conversation to my husband. I wish every girl would have an accountability partner (your parents or a counselor with whom you can share your heart and be confident that it won't go beyond them). Besides helping you as you grow and mature before marriage, that model of communication will help you in your marriage. I'm not saying that learning to communicate with your spouse is always easy, but it's nice to have some practice before you're married.

NEW from Derick . . .

I WANT TO BUILD on what Jill said about communication, and I want to encourage you to cultivate those skills while you're young. Don't wait until it's time to start dating and courting to learn how to have honest conversations. And if I may speak to parents: If you want your children to look up to you their whole lives, that has to start before they're in the middle of a relationship. Whom to marry is the biggest decision of their lives—aside from their decision to follow Christ—and you will want to be involved. The trust thing is huge—keeping confidences between the parents and child and not spreading them around.

NEW from Jessa . . .

NOW THAT WE'RE MARRIED, Ben and I thought we'd share a little of our story: how we met, our courtship, and how we fell in love.

Ben and I first met when his family came up to northwest Arkansas in April 2013. They came to town for a Saturday spring football game and decided to stay the night and come to our church the next day.

Our family was a little late getting to church that morning. I remember walking in with a few of my younger siblings and right off I noticed the "new family." I saw Ben and thought, *Hmm . . . he's a handsome guy.* What stood out to me was his facial hair! It was a cool-looking, kinda anchor-shaped goatee. He looked to be in his early twenties, and I could tell he'd been hitting the gym. We didn't talk much that first Sunday, just exchanged a few words. But I hoped we would meet again.

While up for a visit one weekend, Ben talked with my parents about his feelings for me and asked my parents if he could have permission to get to know me (let's call this a pre-courtship stage). My dad had known Ben for a while and had even talked with him on the phone from time to time. He respected Ben and knew him to be a godly young man.

After a lengthy conversation, Ben headed back to his hometown of Hot Springs with a grin on his face and my phone number added to his contacts! Then the texting began. We were not yet courting, but it was pretty obvious to everyone around that we were interested in each other! Our parents were okay with us talking and getting to know one another as friends, but it was not "an official public relationship" yet.

We kept my parents in the loop by group texting; this way my parents were able to learn more about Ben as well. Our conversations during this stage were very businesslike. Our focus was on asking questions in order to find out more about each other. Could we be compatible as a couple? Did we have the same goals in life? Were we both on the same path, headed in the same direction?

During this time, we became best friends. We were falling in love—though we had yet to actually speak those words to each other! Weeks later, with hundreds of questions asked, Ben once again sat down to talk with my parents, and Ben asked them for permission to court me. It was now official!

During the courtship phase, our relationship became romantic!

Sharing one of our (Jessa & Ben's) first kisses
on our wedding day, November 1, 2014!

This is when we began to express our love for one another. For the first time we spoke the words "I love you!" How sweet those words sound! Ben was the true romantic! He would write sweet letters and poetry, and take me on special dates. He would bring me flowers and chocolates. I am a little less flowery myself, but as time went on, I do think that his "romantic-ness" began to rub off on me! We simply loved being together!

Now that Ben and I are married, we are getting to know each other in deeper and richer ways. We are both thankful for the guidance our parents gave and the examples they have been—and still are—for us. It is our prayer that we continue to grow closer to each other and to God.

MAKING SEVEN KEY COMMITMENTS

HERE ARE SEVEN KEY commitments you can make that will enable you to give your love life to God.

1. I will not date or court anyone who does not love Jesus as much as I do.
2. I will patiently wait on God's timing to bring the man He has for me.
3. I will choose to save my body as a gift for my future spouse.
4. I will choose to not fill my mind with sensual material (R-rated movies or vulgar TV shows, bad Internet sites, teen magazines, and romance novels).
5. I will choose wise friends and wholesome activities.
6. I will share my heart and inward struggles regularly with my parents (or a loving Christian counselor).
7. I will give my love life to God and focus my time and energy on serving the Lord.

God has great things in mind for you. It's up to us to wait on Him and trust His wisdom.

6

YOUR RELATIONSHIP WITH CULTURE

Making choices that will keep you pure

> The eyes of the Lord are in every place,
> beholding the evil and the good.
> —Proverbs 15:3

I N THE PRECEDING CHAPTERS, we've talked about our relationships with *people*—with ourselves, our parents, our siblings, our friends, and with guys. In the next three chapters, we'll talk about our relationship with our culture, our country, and the world. We'll start off with our relationship with culture and how our family chooses our movies and music, and also how we have chosen to use one of the greatest inventions in modern history, the Internet.

THE INTERNET

WITH JUST A FEW clicks of a keyboard, the Internet gives us the ability to research any subject. But it also has the potential to destroy the souls of those who get entangled in its dark side. Mom reminds us that it is not a matter of *if* but *when* Satan will try to tempt us to read or look at something we shouldn't. So, as a family, we have taken some precautionary measures to help us avoid the traps and snares of the enemy.

Accountability

Internet access on our computers and smartphones is controlled by passwords that Mom and we older girls are responsible for. Whenever access is given to the Internet, we keep it in an open area, usually with at least one other person present for accountability. That family guideline was put in place many years ago to protect our family members from accidentally (or even intentionally) browsing to harmful sites that might include pornography or other things that could be detrimental.

Self-Control

Self-control is just as important—if not more so—than being accountable to someone else. When you're in a situation where you think

Our family rule is that anyone accessing the open Internet needs to have Mom or an older sister type in the password, and then computers are kept in prominent places where they are easily visible to all.

you're alone and no one else would ever know, if you have godly self-control, you will still choose to do what is right.

So ask yourself: would your Internet choices be the same when you were all alone as they would be when someone were sitting beside you? Luke 12:2 says, "For there is nothing covered, that shall not be revealed; neither hid, that shall not be known." Dad always reminds us, "When our lives are over and we stand before God, we will have to give an account for everything we did during our lives. And the things we think we're doing in secret will one day be projected up on the big screen for the whole world to see." It's vital to remember that God is always watching. As the Bible tells us, "The eyes of the Lord are in every place, beholding the evil and the good" (Proverbs 15:3).

In reality, we are nothing more than who we are and what we do when we think no one else is watching. That is the real us.

Choices About Time

Many people ask us about our family's take on social media. The TLC network has set up a Facebook account for *19 Kids and Counting* that is used to notify viewers of things related to our family's show, but other than that, at this point we have chosen not to do personal social networking such as Facebook, Twitter, Instagram, etc. (But there are plenty of fake accounts out there under all of our names!) While there is nothing inherently wrong with social networking and it is possible for these things to be used as a tool for ministry, they can often be big time-wasters as people become glued to their electronic world.

Time is one of the greatest resources God gives us, and we should all strive to be good caretakers of it. How often do we sit down at the computer or pull out our smartphone with the thought that we will be on it for just a few minutes? And before we know it, we've spent an hour or two instead—often causing us to neglect other things we needed to accomplish during that time. In Ephesians 5, Paul reminds us, "See then that ye walk circumspectly, not as fools, but as wise, redeeming the time, because the days are evil." To *redeem the time* really means to be a good steward and make the highest and best use of our time. We should be careful to evaluate and consider the time we devote to these things so that it doesn't get out of hand.

Online Flirtations

We realize that social networking can sometimes become an avenue to begin communicating with people we normally would not be in touch with. But we should always be aware of our actions in this regard. Personally, we are very careful not to text, e-mail, or communicate over the Internet with guys on a personal, intimate level. Instead it is wise to keep these interactions businesslike.

Sometimes even just the thought of a guy texting you or chatting with you through the Internet world can make you think, *Maybe he likes me!* But remember, when a young man who has no commitment or obligation to you is flirting with you through texting or the like, it's probable that he is also flirting with many other girls in the same

While the Internet can be a useful source of information, it can also be a danger. Mom has made it a point to teach us about Christ-like character qualities such as self-control, often from the IBLP Wisdom Booklets.

way—and even at the same time. We've seen this time and again. A girl in this situation should ask herself, *Is this really the kind of guy I want?*

Girls who marry this type of guy soon realize that a guy with a flirtatious mind-set cannot suddenly, upon marriage, break his old patterns and habits. Unfortunately, a guy like this cannot safely be trusted, and his flirtations will continue to cause problems and insecurities long into a marriage. If you desire a guy whose heart is fully committed to you, guard your heart against counterfeit love so you can fully give it to Mr. Right at the right time in the right way. (More about relationships with boys in chapter 5.)

Harmful Gossip

One other big issue we've witnessed in the social media world is that some people get hooked on reading gossip and then post their own slanderous statements about others, whom they sometimes don't even know. Or they post something they would never say to that person face-to-face. It comes across as though those posters have nothing better to do with their time.

We've heard that some discussion boards or chat rooms might be better named *bitter rooms* because those drawn to them often seem rather bitter. Possibly they're harboring resentment for circumstances or hurts in their own lives. And since bitter people seem to gravitate toward other bitter people, these sites seem to be the place to hang out. Misery loves company. Unfortunately, some people seem to derive much pleasure from nit-picking other people's lives.

In the Bible, a gossiper is called a *talebearer*, and we're told, "A talebearer revealeth secrets; but he that is of a faithful spirit concealeth the matter" (Proverbs 11:13). Mom taught us the definition of the word *gossip* as "sharing private information with those who are not a part of the problem or a part of the solution." And we also learned that *slander* is "sharing information with a design to hurt." Both gossip and slander are wrong in God's eyes.

Frequently, people involved in online gossip don't know or understand what is going on in a situation, but they are quick to publicly take up offenses or offer judgment or opinion about someone based on what they hear or read. And often, the source of information is not reliable and may be slanted or even altogether false.

Dad has told us that people who put others down often feel they are elevating themselves with an attitude of "I would *never* do what so-and-so did!" They hope others will think more highly of them, but often the opposite happens. People become uncomfortable and begin to wonder, *What do they say about* me *behind my back?* In the end, put-downs may only serve to turn people away.

Mom reminds us often of the words of Thumper's mother in the story of *Bambi:* "If you can't say somethin' nice, then don't say nothin' at all."

With all this said, we have committed to use the Internet so far as it serves as a tool for good, but we are careful to keep safeguards in place so it doesn't consume our lives. It is important for each of us to pray and ask God not only, "What things would You have me add into my life?" but also, "What things would You have me leave out?" And then we follow where He leads.

MOVIES

GOD CONVICTED MOM AND Dad back in the early days of their marriage not to have broadcast television in the home. Before our parents were married they went through marriage counseling, and the Christian counselor challenged them to make two commitments: the first was not to have a pet for the first year of marriage and the second was not to have a TV for the first year of marriage. They agreed to both, and for the first year of marriage, they say they were living on love.

Right around their first anniversary, someone gave them a TV, and they decided to get cable service hooked up. Over the next few weeks as they sat there, glued to the tube, they began to notice that their verbal communication as a couple had greatly dropped off. And not only that, but they couldn't believe how bad television had gotten in just one year (and this was back in 1985)! They decided they were going to get rid of cable, and we would all say that is one of the best things they have done for our family.

Growing up, we had a small TV and video player in the home, but it was not placed in the center of our living room as a constant call to come, sit down, and be amused and entertained. As the saying goes, out of sight, out of mind. We stored it in a closet and pulled it out on certain occasions. Now we have a video projector and pull-down projector screen mounted from our living room ceiling but still use it sparingly. Bookshelves have been placed in prime locations as an encouragement for us to read, and they are filled with the adventures of missionary stories, history from all eras, and biographies of great men and women.

Creativity vs. Entertainment

Our parents have worked hard to encourage creative mind-sets in us kids, inspiring us to build, grow, and create, rather than having entertainment mind-sets that always need to be watching movies or playing video games. And through their encouragement, we've found the makings of many talented artists, gardeners, inventors, and musicians among us. For example, by age twelve, Jason had successfully experimented with several different types of gardening on his own, including a greenhouse. By age fourteen, Josh was taking apart old computers and rebuilding his own. By age fifteen, Jana was able to sew some quite exquisite costumes and clothing for herself and others. By age ten, John was working on and operating heavy equipment, assisting Dad in building the house we currently live in.

Dad has always told us, "Watching too much TV will dumb you down. It stifles a person's God-given creativity."

While our typical family night usually consists of playing sports or board games together, sharing snacks and lots of good, old-fashioned conversation, we do on occasion enjoy sitting down together as a family and watching a movie. Mom and Dad have always been careful to choose movies that embrace the values that we hold dear, and not ones that would undermine them.

The point is, Duggars do watch movies, but when we do, we are very selective. Some movies are good and wholesome *except for that one part,* and so we try to excuse the bad scene by pointing out the "really good scenes." But Grandma Duggar would compare this to scrambling one rotten egg in with a dozen good eggs. It makes the whole batch bad.

We donned apparel from the biblical age to sail the Sea of Galilee while we were visiting Israel.

Dangerous Influences

When we let "little things" slide by, we become desensitized to them. This applies to any area of life, not just movies. Eventually, when we let the little things slide, the things that once bothered our conscience will no longer affect us because our conscience has been seared. If we sense this happening in our family, we may go on a "movie fast," where we will refrain from watching movies for a month or so. We have found that after doing this, we are usually much more sensitive to the message of a film and have a renewed sense of balance.

Much of the Hollywood and pop culture media glorifies things that God considers to be wicked, and younger and younger audiences are exposed to those things as being acceptable. Movies with suggestive themes and foul language that are now "rated G for the whole family" would have gotten a stricter rating just a few years ago.

One specific thing that our parents have always been careful about is magic, which often shows up in children's movies. As harmless as it may seem, it's not a joke in God's eyes. Magic, sorcery, witches, spell-casting, and the like are all part of a demonic realm that God wants us to stay away from. No matter how "good" a film containing magic may seem, God speaks seriously about this throughout the Bible; it is not something to be glorified or portrayed by any means as something fun or attractive.

Another troublesome thing in today's films is much more subtle: bad attitudes and disrespect. We see children mouthing off to their parents and living in direct disobedience to authorities. Too often, dads are portrayed as dummies, moms as overbearing, and grandparents as old-fashioned. It is no wonder the youth culture today is the way it is. Television is being used as a babysitter and a way to keep kids occupied, but often parents don't realize it is a *teacher* and that kids are like sponges, soaking up everything they are being taught. Parents say, "I don't want you talking to me like that!" but then they turn right around and set their kids down in front of a television screen where they are being taught that this behavior is acceptable and the way to be "cool."

Making Wise Choices

If we are in the middle of a movie and something bad comes up unexpectedly, Mom and Dad are quick to say, "That's not good." Sometimes we even pause the movie and discuss how we should never use God's name carelessly like they did in the movie, or Mom or Dad will ask, "Did you see how that boy responded to his dad? That was disrespectful." Mom and Dad use discernment as to whether or not we continue watching the film. If they did choose to continue the movie, if wrong ideas, attitudes, and behaviors were promoted, we would most likely shut it off and be done with the movie. And definitely if there were any themes of sorcery or immorality, it would be game over.

Our family loves traveling together. We had fun stopping by the Hollywood Wax Museum in Branson, Missouri, and posing for a quick family picture.

We love to watch educational documentaries that teach about science and history from a biblical perspective, and we also enjoy films such as *Courageous, Fireproof, Flywheel,* and *Facing the Giants*—all of which promote the values our family strives to uphold. From time to time we also enjoy watching many of the old classics that promote honesty, respect of parents, and reverence for God. One of our family favorites is undoubtedly *Sergeant York.* But even in that one, we don't approve of the scene where he and his girlfriend kiss before they're married.

We have enjoyed many carefully selected episodes of *The Andy Griffith Show* as long as they are not centered around a lot of romance or deceptiveness, as some of them are. Also it is important to realize even though a "clean" show may not have anything outright bad in it, it may contain an indirect hidden message. Ask yourself, *Are the people watching this show being taught to turn to God and His principles through the story lines, or are they learning to live their lives without God's guidance and do whatever is right in their own eyes?*

Basically, we can't give a blanket stamp of approval to anything because there will usually be at least one or two things we disagree with in any given film. However, we encourage you to personally evaluate the television and movies you watch and, as Grandma encourages us to do, ask yourself, *Is this something God would be pleased with?*

MUSIC

FOR CHRISTIANS, THIS AREA requires much prayerful consideration. It's not our goal to give a specific list of all the albums we listen to, but we will share how we choose our music and mention some of our personal preferences. Growing up, our parents explained to us that if we, as Christians, accept music that promotes the very things God hates, we bring a blot to the name and character of the God we represent.

The first thing we do in deciding if a song should be played in our home is to determine the message of the lyrics. Soon after Mom became a Christian at the age of fifteen, a friend encouraged her to write out the lyrics of questionable songs and then compare them to the truths found in the Bible. For instance, if a song's lyrics are saying, "Follow your heart. Do what feels good," we compare it to the Bible and find that God says, "The heart is deceitful above all things, and desperately wicked" (Jeremiah 17:9). So we know, based on the Bible, that we're not supposed to follow our hearts, as that will only get us in trouble. Instead of *following* our hearts, we should *lead* our hearts; and instead of doing what "feels good," we should make sure we are doing what God wants us to do.

Clearly, if a song's lyrics are glorifying sensuality, immorality, disrespect, violence, suicide, or the use of drugs and alcohol, we have good reason to avoid it. These things are often spoken of or hinted at in the lines of country music, but if we were to point to one genre, it would be rock 'n' roll and its variations such as hard rock and heavy metal. We avoid these types of music altogether. Since its beginnings in the 1950s, this music's main goal and purpose have been to promote every

Our family definitely enjoys music! Here we are in
Ireland, drumming on traditional budhrans.

one of the issues we want to avoid. A heavy backbeat and words being sung in a breathy and sensual voice—and even the style of rock 'n' roll music itself—give off an attitude of rebellion, resistance toward authority, and a rejection of morality. None of these things come without consequences. As we have examined the lives of many of these artists, we have seen the outcome of such living. It was sad to find that on average, the life expectancy for rock artists and musicians is around forty; many of them die at a young age for reasons related to AIDS, drug or alcohol abuse, or suicides. It's a tragic reality.

Our family does not support the idea of Christians adopting this type of music or putting "Christian words" to it and bringing it into the church, because the underlying message of the music is still the same, and we believe that the combination of the two sends a mixed message. Our God is not the author of confusion but of order, and our lives and even our music should be a reflection of that. We have found that classical music and traditional hymns usually follow a pattern and maintain a very distinct and definite order, and over the years Mom and Dad have encouraged us to pursue those types of music.

Even though our parents did not have any kind of musical training, they wanted their children to have the opportunity to learn music, so early on, they arranged for us to take both piano and violin lessons. Since then, many of us have branched out and taken up other instruments such as guitar, mandolin, bass, cello, viola, trumpet, and harp.

Given the basic guidelines that we follow for selecting music, there is still plenty of musical variety in the Duggar household these days. We enjoy listening to Celtic, mountain, bluegrass, and gospel music as well as orchestrated marches and classical pieces. Just as our parents have encouraged us, we exhort you to hold the area of your music with an open hand, and to pray about and be willing to give up anything you feel would not be pleasing to God.

On a final note, Duggars do not make a habit of walking around listening to music with earbuds in, as if to block out everything around them and retract into their own little private world. It's one thing if we are mowing the lawn or doing some kind of work project on our own, but otherwise Dad will encourage us, "If it's good enough for you to listen to, why don't we all listen to it!"

God has called us to be light and salt in the world we live in. As we make our own choices based on His Word and principles, our prayer is that we will be a light to others as they make choices of their own.

7

Your Relationship with Your Country

Making a difference in the political arena

> *. . . For there is no power but of God:*
> *The powers that be are ordained of God.*
> —Romans 13:1

GOD USED A SERIES of supernatural events to clearly lead our family into making a difference in the world of politics. And it's a path that our family firmly believes in and has thoroughly enjoyed. It all began with a rally on the steps of the Arkansas capitol in 1997. We had traveled three hours to Little Rock for our infant brother Josiah's doctor appointment. A few days before, Dad had heard on a Christian radio station that a rally was going to be held at the state capitol a few hours after Josiah's scheduled appointment. The focus of the rally was to urge the legislature to pass a ban against the heinous procedure of partial-birth abortion.

Mom and Dad decided that since we were in town, we would

stop by the rally. When we got there, what we saw was inspiring: more than two thousand people were passionately advocating for the lives of these innocent, almost full-term babies whose lives were being destroyed through this gruesome act. But despite the large turnout and urgent pleas, instead of passing the ban, the representatives and senators voted it down!

That day changed our lives.

Dad says that as he watched those events unfold, God laid it on his heart to run for the legislature. He'd never been involved in politics, didn't consider himself a public speaker, and honestly didn't know the first thing about running a campaign. But he knew he could vote the right way on life-and-death issues, which was better than what most of our elected officials at the capitol were doing.

A few weeks later, when Dad heard about a candidate campaign class that a Christian man was going to teach, Dad was one of the first to sign up. However, during the first training session, the instructor announced his plans to run for the very representative seat Dad was considering. For a moment, Dad was shocked. Had he heard wrong? Was God really calling him to this?

In some ways he actually felt a bit relieved that God had provided someone else who Dad knew was a very qualified, Christian man to run for this office instead of him. He felt sure God had just been testing him to see if he was willing to do whatever He asked him to do. Nonetheless, Dad enjoyed learning about campaign strategies, so he returned to the class the next week.

Imagine his surprise when he heard the instructor say that he had just taken a job out of town, and he would no longer be able to run for the representative seat! Even though Dad still felt totally inadequate, he became even more convinced this was what God was calling him to do, and he filed to run for office.

Over the next several months, God kept confirming to him through little circumstances that this was what He wanted Dad to do.

For instance, during this time a family friend asked if she could introduce our family to a young couple in need of some encouragement. Mom and Dad worked out a time the following week to have them over for supper, and during some delightful conversation with these new friends, Dad mentioned the direction God was leading him—to run for office. We were unaware that this man's forte was graphic design and printing—until he graciously offered to help us put together Dad's campaign cards!

Family photos were taken, and a few days later we were holding in our hands a professionally designed campaign card with our family picture on the front and, on the back, a message explaining the values Dad stood for. With several thousand of these printed up, Dad, Mom, Grandma Duggar, and a handful of friends began canvassing our legis-

By the time we took this photo in front of the U.S. Capitol, there were eleven Duggar kids, including the second set of twins, Jeremiah and Jedidiah.

lative district, always with one or more of us kids in tow, knocking on doors and talking with the voters.

While most people were kind and gracious, some were not, and in those cases they were not afraid to speak their minds. The newspapers that interviewed Dad had already endorsed his Democrat opponent, and we began to notice that the articles they published about Dad were negative and slanted.

Dad told us he went up to one house and knocked, and when a lady came to the door, he said, "Hi, I am Jim Bob Duggar, and I'm running for the office of state representa—"

The lady immediately cut in and, obviously not of the same opinion when it comes to family size and children being considered a blessing from God, she said, "I know who you are, and I am not going to vote for you until you get a vasectomy!" Then she slammed the door in his face.

Another incident occurred after a long day of campaign work when Mom called up one of our favorite hometown restaurants to order pizzas for supper. When she gave them her name, the employee on the other end of the line recognized who she was and told her, "Your husband is going to lose—and lose *bad!*"

But because Mom and Dad knew this was what God had called our family to do, they didn't let things like that discourage them; instead it reminded them to continue praying and trusting God. During family Bible time one evening, we discussed how being constantly worried about what other people think about us can hinder us from doing what is right. We prayed together as a family, giving God our reputation.

In giving our family's reputation to God, Mom and Dad were, in essence, saying, "God, we care what You think about us over anyone else, and no matter what other people may say against us, we are willing to keep doing what You have called us to do." This freed us from those feelings of wanting to be people-pleasers, and instead set our focus back on faithfully doing what we knew God had asked of us.

Little did any of us know what God had in store.

When the votes were counted, Dad won with 56 percent of the vote.

Our parents rented a house near Little Rock to live in while the legislature was in session, and Dad took some of us kids along each day to the capitol. We worked on our homeschool assignments while we sat in committee meetings or watched the proceedings from the House gallery. It was a wonderful, hands-on homeschool experience for us all.

The next election cycle, Dad was reelected to a second term in the House of Representatives, and during that time he had another "lightning bolt" moment. This time he felt God urging him to run for the US Senate.

By then, we Duggar kids felt we were old hands at campaigning. Usually accompanied by our parents or Grandma Duggar, we rang doorbells, passed out leaflets at county fairs, rode in parades, and asked people to vote for Dad every chance we got. We even wrote and recorded our own jingle for Dad's statewide campaign.

And then, he lost.

We had worked hard, despite the fact that we were outspent by our opponent twenty to one. But even though he didn't win, Dad said he knew beyond a shadow of a doubt that God had called him to run for the national office. "God called us to run, but He didn't promise we would win," Dad told us. "As John Quincy Adams said, 'Duty is ours; results are up to God.' I know we did what God asked of us."

Dad led us in a prayer of thanksgiving for leading us through the race—and even thanked Him for the outcome. Then, at the end of the prayer, he said, "Lord, we are ready for our next assignment!"

One Thing Leads to Another . . .

AS WE WERE FOLLOWING God's leading with our political involvement, God opened up another—and very unexpected—door of influence. On Election Day, Mom and Dad had taken all of us kids along when they went to vote. They try to use everyday events as part of our home-school training, and on that particular day, Mom had said that voting would serve as a civics class field trip for all of us Duggar children.

It just so happened that an Associated Press photographer was at the polling place and took a picture of all of us (we numbered thirteen at the time) as we walked into the voting precinct. Dad later jokingly said, "If all the kids had been old enough to vote, I would have won by a large margin!"

Our family found out later that the photo was picked up by the *New York Times*, which ran it with a caption identifying a US Senate

During Dad's campaigns we loved dressing in red and
making appearances together as a family.

candidate in Arkansas walking in to vote with his wife and their thirteen kids. A freelance writer saw the photo and wrote a story about our
family that later appeared in *Parents* magazine, where it was noticed by
Eileen O'Neill, the president of the Discovery Health Channel. She
asked Bill Hayes with Figure 8 Films to call and ask Mom and Dad if
they could do a one-hour documentary about our family.

As with every major decision, our family prayed together about
this one and sought wise, godly counsel. Mom and Dad believed this
could be an avenue to share with the world their strong belief that
children are a blessing from God, and believed it could be a way to encourage families to draw closer to Him and to each other. They told
the network we would allow them to do the documentary as long as
they didn't edit out our faith in God, because that is the core of our
lives.

The executives agreed, saying, "It's your story. You can tell it."

While they were filming the show, Mom became pregnant with
our fifteenth sibling, Jackson, and he was born on the show. The name
of that first show was *14 Children and Pregnant Again.* It aired in 2004,
pulling in what network officials said was one of the biggest audiences
in Discovery Health Channel's history. That first documentary led to
another, which led to another, and another. After the fifth documentary
the network asked if they could film a reality TV *series* with us.

We had never even heard of that type of show, but we agreed to
do it based upon our hope that it would enable our family to share encouraging Bible principles with many other people. We filmed a series called *17 Kids and Counting.* Then Mom had another baby, and
the name was changed to *18 Kids and Counting.* Then to *19 Kids and
Counting,* which now airs on The Learning Channel (TLC).

When Mom and Dad were asked to do the first documentary,
none of us dreamed that it would turn into more than two hundred
shows in ten years. We are powerfully encouraged by the hundreds
of letters and e-mails we receive each week from families all over

196 | Growing Up Duggar

the world who have shared how their lives have been spiritually challenged by watching the shows. Many couples have told us they have started taking their family to church. We've learned of fathers who have started leading their family in Bible time each evening. We've even heard about abortions that have been canceled as women have decided to view their child for what it truly is—a blessing from God!

Hearing about the TV show's history often leads to the next frequently asked question: "What's it like growing up with TV cameras around your house all the time? Is it difficult?"

Well, first off, they are not around all the time. On average, our production crew usually films two or three days a week for two or three hours per day. The members of the film crew have become our dear friends, as close to us as family, as they have been a part of almost every major family event during the last several years. They were there when some of us older kids got our wisdom teeth pulled, and when the majority of our family got *really* ill with motion sickness during a sightseeing flight over the Grand Canyon. They cheered us on as we precariously boarded a jet boat for a wild ride up the Niagara River as well as when a few of us were determined to brave the twelve-thousand-foot jump out of a skydiving airplane.

The cameras have captured a lot of smiles and laughter over the years, including a zillion birthday parties and quite a few births, weddings, and some pretty exciting adventures all over the world. But the cameras have also continued to roll as we've struggled through challenge and heartache. They recorded the fear we faced when Josie was born several months early and Mom came closer to dying than any of us wanted to think about. And they were there when we grieved over Grandpa Duggar's illness with brain cancer and also when he passed away. They were there for his funeral. And when we lost baby Jubilee in 2012, our grief was once again shared with millions of viewers.

Even though these were very difficult times for us, we prayed that God would somehow use our sorrow and that others would see what a difference having faith in Jesus Christ can make when we go through hard times. As Scripture says, we don't grieve as though who have no hope. We have seen that God used these times to draw us closer to Him and to each other, and we are comforted knowing that, without a doubt, we will see these loved ones again someday in heaven.

Our desire is to build family unity and a oneness of spirit, which comes as we work to apply God's principles to our daily lives. We look at the television show as our family ministry and as an opportunity to tell of God's greatness and His love to those we might otherwise never have the opportunity to meet.

Meanwhile, the show aims to satisfy the curiosity of the general public by providing an inside look at how a supersized family operates—from daily mounds of dirty laundry, dishes, and homeschool assignments, to the impending adventures that are certain to occur with any family outing or road trip. Throughout the years, our prayer has remained that people will see that it is only by God's grace that our

We've grown up in front of the cameras filming our cable TV series
19 Kids and Counting. This photo was taken when we kids did
our first TV interview with a local reporter back in 2000.

large but otherwise ordinary family can maintain strong relationships with one another and pull together through challenges big and small.

It's interesting to see how everything is linked—how one response to God's calling leads to another: God prompted Dad to run for political office, and because of his obedience there, God continued to lead by opening other doors of ministry. Even though we will not always understand God's leading at first, it's vital that we follow where His Word guides us, regardless of the opposition that comes our way. Otherwise we will miss out on the opportunities He's providing to be a witness for Him.

OUR CONTINUED INVOLVEMENT IN POLITICS

DAD'S LOSS IN THAT Senate campaign did not end our involvement in politics. During the last few years we have been more involved than ever, and we've enjoyed helping behind the scenes with campaigns of conservative Christians running for office.

We believe that our freedoms to vote for and support the candidates of our choosing are not something to be taken lightly. We're thankful to God and to all the soldiers who have fought and died to keep those freedoms alive. We believe it's our duty as citizens to get out and vote on Election Day and show our gratitude.

If you have never been involved in helping a campaign, you are missing out on a lot of fun! We all love it. So here's what you need to do:

First, if you are eighteen or older, go register to vote.

Second, find a conservative Christian who is running for office and then call and ask them where he or she stands on the issues.

Third, check the candidate's past voting record to see if it matches what you were told about his or her stand.

Fourth, if those answers are satisfactory, volunteer to help in the candidate's campaign. You don't have to know much in advance because you will get on-the-job training (making phone calls, putting up yard signs, organizing events).

Fifth, when you're old enough to run for office, pray about taking up that challenge to make a difference.

Patriot Academy and TeenPact are two excellent organizations that teach young people about the godly principles America was founded on and how government is supposed to work.

Since Dad's first experience in politics, our family has worked together to investigate and support candidates who share our conservative Christian beliefs. Almost every election cycle, we campaign for local and state candidates the same way we campaigned when Dad was running: we walk the neighborhoods, ringing doorbells to encourage residents to vote for our candidate.

One evening many years ago during Dad's first campaign, some families met up at our house to divide into teams for some neighborhood canvassing. We don't celebrate Halloween, and everyone totally forgot what day it was—October 31. So that evening as we girls walked through the neighborhood with an adult, all of us wearing our ruffly dresses and hair ribbons and carrying our bags of campaign leaflets, people were offering us candy and telling us they loved our dresses. We eventually caught on and suspended our campaigning efforts till the next morning, but that day we received the friendliest greetings ever while knocking on doors during a campaign season!

More than fourteen years later, in 2012, we older siblings stepped up our political work and took campaigning to the next level. First we met as a family to talk about which presidential candidate shared our values and beliefs. We older kids, along with Mom and Dad, had done our research, and we all discussed the various candidates, what they believed in and what values they would be promoting as president. We prayed, asking God to guide us in making our choice. We studied the real issues, the candidates' core values, and their voting records. We talked about which person, running for the highest elected office in our country, would have the backbone to stand for what is right?

If we were going to endorse someone, we really wanted to make sure the person we chose was someone whose core beliefs and philosophy agreed with our own. Everyone knows that politics can be a dirty, misleading business. We've all seen candidates who say one thing but then do another when they're elected.

After lots of prayer, research, and discussion, as a family, we all agreed that Rick Santorum, a Republican former US senator from Pennsylvania, was a presidential candidate we could fully endorse. We admired his courage and confidence, and we especially like that he had the courage to author the bill that finally ended partial-birth abortions in America. (If you remember from the beginning of this chapter, this was the very issue God used to bring our family into politics back in 1997.)

With the Iowa caucuses about a week away, we knew we had to work quickly. Dad said that with so many candidates in the race, he expected that this election would be very close. We discussed the idea of gathering some friends from the area and driving up to Iowa to lend a hand, and Dad added jokingly, "Maybe our mobile support team could help put Santorum over the top!"

Dad called the Santorum campaign headquarters, where the staff said they could gladly use as many volunteers as we would bring. Dad asked where the candidate would be appearing in the next few days. We called some friends we knew who would be up for a last-minute adventure and invited them to jump on the bus, as we would be heading to Iowa the next morning.

As we hit the road that morning, our team totaled twenty-six people, including Dad, several of the older Duggar kids, and many friends. We arrived in Iowa about 1:30 A.M. and settled into a hotel near where Senator Santorum was to appear that day.

We got a little sleep, and the next morning, Dad went down to the hotel lobby and phoned one of the campaign staff members to say we had brought a big group from out of state to help in the campaign and we were ready to get busy. While Dad was on the phone, he was surprised to see Rick Santorum himself walk into the hotel lobby. We had no clue he was staying in the same hotel.

Dad approached the senator and introduced himself, telling him we had brought reinforcements from Arkansas to help him in his campaign. Senator Santorum expressed gratefulness and said we could meet him at his next event.

One of the first campaign stops we attended with him was a meet-and-greet at a coffee shop. We pulled our bus up out front, and all of us came swarming out to stir up enthusiasm for the candidate's appearance. More than a hundred journalists from all over the world had showed up at that coffee shop that morning, and when we pulled up, several reporters recognized our family. Dad started doing one interview after another, saying our family had driven up from Arkansas to get the word out that Rick Santorum was the conservative Christian candidate that our family was getting behind and we were asking others to join us in supporting him. Dad went on to share how Senator Rick Santorum had authored the bill to ban partial-birth abortion in America and that he knew Rick would stand for what is right.

Our younger sister Joy was happy to chauffeur US senator Rick Santorum around our home while little brother Justin served as tour guide.

Dad said over and over again that Rick Santorum has a backbone of steel and a heart of gold.

At a later event, Senator Santorum told supporters he had been (and still was) driving all over Iowa in a pickup truck, campaigning on a shoestring budget. But when he pulled up to the hotel that morning, the first thing he saw was a huge bus covered with "Rick Santorum for President." He assumed his staff had gone out and leased a very expensive bus for his campaign, and he was incredulous, demanding, "Who authorized the money for that bus? We don't have money to spend on this sort of thing!"

His staff reassured him they had not spent a dime on the bus and that it belonged to a group of volunteers who had brought their own bus to help out. When we heard this, we all had a good laugh!

We attended several Santorum campaign appearances in Iowa, and as his crowds grew, the need for a sound system became apparent. Josh and John went to Radio Shack and bought a small portable karaoke-style amplifier for the candidate to use.

We continued to go from one rally to the next, the twenty-six of us serving as a mobile support team, cheering and handing out literature wherever he spoke. We were delighted to see his poll numbers going up—not because of our work on his behalf but because people were learning what he stood for and liking what they saw.

On January 3, 2012, Santorum ended up losing the Iowa caucuses by eight votes. *Eight!* We rode back home to Arkansas thinking, *Oh, man! We should have worked just a little harder.* We were disappointed, but we also saw that our candidate had tremendous momentum, and we still wanted to help. (Later in January, the official recount tally showed that Santorum had actually *won* the Iowa caucuses by thirty-four votes, increasing his campaign's momentum even more.) If they got overly disruptive, our older brothers, along with some of the boys in the Bates family, who had joined us, would gently but firmly edge the glitter bombers out of the crowd.

Two weeks before the South Carolina primary, Jessa, Jinger, and I (Jill), along with our brother John-David, loaded up the bus and took off for South Carolina. It was the first time we kids had taken the family bus on the road campaigning by ourselves. Other friends came along—not as many as before but enough to make another small but energetic mobile support team when needed.

At first we made calls from the campaign headquarters and served as an advance team, putting out signs and helping make sure things were ready before the candidate's appearances.

As time went on, Santorum had a multitude of requests to hold rallies in many different states. Because he could only be in one place at a time, our team was able to join with local volunteers to hold separate events and speak on Santorum's behalf. Grandma and Jana volunteered to hold down the fort one weekend so that Dad and Mom could come to South Carolina and help out. They did a couple of events with the candidate, and we Duggar kids did some on our own.

As the campaign grew, so did the size of the crowds—and the challenges. We would help set things up, have signs ready to hand out to supporters, hand out literature, and give media interviews when asked.

We had studied the candidate and knew what he stood for, so we were happy to share when people asked about Santorum's stand on lowering taxes, improving education, strengthening families, and pro-life issues.

Santorum's campaign had attracted negative attention as well as positive, and we quickly learned to recognize the people who showed up to cause disruptions and "glitter bomb" the candidate and crowd, throwing red and green glitter all over everyone. Until his campaign grew large enough to have its own security team, we helped with those jobs, too. When we saw the glitter bombers at a rally we would keep an eye on them and notify the police officers working at the event of what they most likely would do.

At one rally, I (Jill) was standing next to an older man, a very wealthy Iowa banker who had come out to support Santorum. I saw the glitter bombers making their move but not in time to warn the gentleman, and he got covered in green glitter. He was pretty upset! I'm not sure what the glitter bombers' goal was, but if they were trying to win people over to their side, it wasn't working.

We lived on the bus for several weeks during that time and actually got pretty good at understanding how truck stops work (although we never got over the sense of feeling like prisoners whenever they called our number for our turn in the shower).

In all, we campaigned for Santorum in ten states: Iowa, South Carolina, Florida, Alabama, Louisiana, Missouri, Oklahoma, Illinois, Michigan, and Wisconsin, living on the bus everywhere except Michigan.

It was exciting, exhausting work—and very rewarding to watch the campaign grow from tiny stops in Iowa, where only a handful of voters showed up, and then to be thrust into a massive movement complete with professional-level event preparation, Secret Service presence, and a media frenzy wherever he showed up.

Our goal was to get the word out that Santorum was the family-values candidate everyone should get behind. We said that over and over wherever we went on the campaign trail.

Everyone on the campaign worked hard, but by early April, it was apparent that the vote had been split by other candidates running in the Republican primary and Santorum wasn't going to gain enough delegates to put him over the top. In the first week of April, Dad was part of a conference call when the campaign team was told the campaign might be coming to an end. On April 10, 2012, Santorum made it official. His campaign had endured some losses and other setbacks—including his young daughter Bella's near-fatal illness back home—and he pulled out of the race.

We were sad, but also grateful for all the experiences we'd shared in helping with a national campaign. We made many memories along the way, and we look forward to the next race.

Later in 2012, we were able to be a part of several local senate and representative races; many of the candidates we supported are now in office. You win some, you lose some. In the end it depends on the hearts of the voters. All we can do is get involved and do our part.

Our desire is to impact the world for God through the political scene. I (Jill) get energized by this work. We joke that it runs in our blood! I am willing to speak in front of crowds, while others in our family would rather avoid that part. But we can all get involved in one way or another.

Jana, Jessa, and Jinger are happier being part of the crowd, handing out literature, chatting with the people who show up, working the phone banks, and taking care of behind-the-scenes duties. (Plus, our fearless sister Jana is right at home driving the bus—and although some of us have done it here and there, we're happiest turning that job over to Jana and the guys!)

When we volunteered to help Senator Rick Santorum in his presidential campaign, Jinger was often called on to take campaign photos, but occasionally she found herself on the other side of the lens.

Some people think Christians should stay out of the political arena, but we strongly disagree. Our family believes faith and politics should go hand in hand, and we've seen countless examples of how that happens. For example, earlier this year, the Arkansas legislature passed one of the most restrictive abortion laws in the country, banning all abortions after twelve weeks' gestation—even overriding the governor's veto to make it final. The effort was led by conservative Christian legislators who campaigned on the principles they believed and then followed through when they were elected.

Our nation was founded on the Bible and on Judeo-Christian principles, and we see it as our responsibility to protect those freedoms by supporting candidates who hold true to those same values and principles. Our prayer is that by sharing our political experiences with others, many will see the need to get involved, and together we can all make a difference!

8

Your Relationship with the World

Developing a servant's heart

> *Let your light so shine before men,*
> *that they may see your good works,*
> *and glorify your Father which is in heaven.*
> —Matthew 5:16

W E'LL NEVER FORGET THE girls in the cage.

Serving Outside the United States

Locked Up and Abandoned

It wasn't the kind of cage you might see at the zoo but a twenty-foot-high fenced area in an orphanage in Central America. Dad and several of us Duggars had traveled with some friends to El Salvador and

Honduras to help and encourage Christians working in ministry there and to do what we could to help spread the gospel. We spent one day visiting a couple of orphanages, and when we came to visit the older girls who live in one government-run facility, we walked through heavy steel doors that clanged shut behind us after we passed. We could hear the security guard threading the heavy chain back through the door handles and snapping the big padlock closed, locking us in with the thirty girls, ages eleven to seventeen, who live in either of the two big rooms joined by a small, center courtyard, sleeping on bunk beds and looking out on the world through iron-barred windows.

They're locked in this high-security area of the orphanage, not because they've done something bad, but because they're thought to have the greatest potential for trying to escape or because they have noncustodial relatives who may want to kidnap them. Ironically, as soon as they turn eighteen, these girls are turned out onto the street, most likely with no skills and no means of supporting themselves.

We were there during the closing days of our latest mission trip to Central America. We had ridden in the back of pickup trucks with local Christian friends and hiked long distances to bring the gospel to residents of remote villages, visiting them in their simple, mud-brick homes. We'd attended church services and helped put on conferences with dedicated believers in area churches. And now we had gotten permission to visit a

In 2013, Dad accompanied most of the older Duggar kids on a missions trip to Honduras, including, from left, Jinger, Jill, Jessa, Jana, and Joy.

government-run orphanage, bringing the girls simple treats and gifts, including Bibles. We'd visited the other areas of the orphanage, including the section where teenage mothers tended their babies, and the areas where younger children lived. Then came the visit to the older "high-risk" girls. The girls in the cage.

We gathered in the center courtyard, which was enclosed by an old, rusty, twenty-foot-high chain-link fence topped with barbed wire. We began with a quick little mime skit and then shared why we had come—to tell them about Jesus. I (Jana) shared my testimony and told the girls God loves each one of them. Through an interpreter, I told them how they could have a relationship with Jesus if they received the gift of salvation and forgiveness He offers to each of us.

Then I asked, "If you were to die tonight, how many think you would go to heaven?"

A few of the girls raised their hands, but many were unsure.

Then I asked, "How many think you will go to hell?"

One girl raised her hand. She wore a black leather jacket—and a sullen, almost angry demeanor. She'd paced nervously while we'd presented the skit and then while I shared my testimony. At one point, she walked away and then came back in.

The next part of our visit was sharing a craft project and making bracelets together, which gave us an opportunity to visit informally one-on-one with the girls. I (Jill) began to help the girl wearing the black jacket make her bracelet, which gave me time to talk with her. While Jana had been talking and the girl had been pacing, I'd prayed fervently that God would calm her spirit and open her heart to the good news we were bringing. I'm working hard to learn Spanish, and I was able to have a simple conversation with her. She told me she'd lived in the orphanage since she was two years old. Her dad was from Guatemala and her mom was from Mexico, she said, "and they don't care about me."

I was able to talk to her about how she could have a personal relationship with Jesus, who *does* care about her. I gave her a little Bible and showed her some key verses. I pointed them out to her and then asked her to read them herself. When I asked if she understood, she nodded. When it was time to leave, I asked her how I could pray for her. She said her prayer was that someday she could meet her mom.

I prayed for her, asking God to bring her mom back into her life. But I prayed in English, which she didn't understand, so I prayed for a lot more than that! I asked God to help her work through the hard things of the past and find healing. And I asked that she would be able to forgive those who had offended her and break the chains of bitterness that seemed to spread such gloom over her. But most important, I prayed that her heart would be softened toward God and that one day she would be saved, remembering what Jesus told His disciples, that sometimes "one soweth, and another reapeth" (John 4:37). In other words, I hoped the seed of the gospel planted in this girl's heart would one day come to fruition—if God would so choose, through another person—and that she would become a powerful example to other girls walking through the same struggles she has known all her life.

Another girl, about fourteen, also left a lasting memory. She cried as she told us she'd been there only six days and she knew she would stay until she was eighteen.

It was hard to leave those girls, and we were all in tears as we said good-bye. It wasn't only their day-to-day situation—in essence, living in a locked cage—that broke our hearts; it

Our most common way of traveling while on our missions trips to Central America is standing with others in the back of a pickup truck, holding on to the enclosing metal framework. Only the bravest travelers stand on the back bumper!

was that we knew that, aside from Jesus, they had no hope. They longed to escape from the orphanage, but at the same time they knew they had little chance for a better life outside its walls. Many had been taken out of abusive situations, but now the system that was set up to protect them was creating a different kind of abuse.

Shalom Children's Home

From there we traveled to another orphanage, this one run by Christians from the States, and it was completely opposite to the sad facility we had visited earlier. The children there were happy—and loved. In fact, one of the challenges the Christian orphanage was facing was that children who grew up there and turned eighteen didn't want to leave! The couple who ran the orphanage accommodated those requests by giving the former residents jobs at the orphanage or letting them live there while they volunteered their services. But two weeks before our visit, government officials had told the owners the "children" had to leave when they turned eighteen—no exceptions. It was a heartbreaking situation for everyone involved.

There was a lot of sadness and heartache in the places we visited in Central America, but the Christian orphanage, Shalom Children's Home, also was a place of great inspiration, especially when we heard the story of the Americans who started it.

Don and Rose Ann Benner had enjoyed a comfortable life in Colorado, where Don worked as an executive for an international corporation. In 1976, when Don was fifty-two, the Benners felt called to do missionary work in foreign lands, and they sold their home and possessions and traveled by land with their two children to Costa Rica, where Don spent a year in language school, learning Spanish. They asked God to show them where He wanted them to go—and that prayer led them to El Salvador.

You can read their amazing story in full at their website,

hisdonations.com, but to keep things short, in 1983 they started Sha-lom Children's Home with thirteen children who had been orphaned during El Salvador's long civil war. Since then they've welcomed hundreds of other children into their love-filled facility, and they've also opened a Christian school and now operate feeding facilities for area residents in need. Their work is totally supported by donations—and by groups of volunteers who come from America and other countries to help.

We've worked in children's shelters here in Arkansas as well as those in Central America. We also visited an orphanage last year during our visit to China (more about that later). Our family is drawn to children's facilities in part because God says true ministry is visiting the widows and fatherless, and also because of the stories Mom's father, our Grandpa Ruark, told us about the years when he and three siblings lived in an orphanage.

Grandpa's father died at a young age during the Great Depression, and his mother wasn't able to earn enough money to provide for her children. She had no choice but to put them in a children's home. After a short while, Grandpa's sister was placed in a loving foster home, but Grandpa and his brother and other sister lived in the orphanage eight long years, until their mother remarried and was able to bring her children home with her again.

Grandpa said it was a hard life, but he was glad to have food and a bed. He told us he was grateful for everything that was done to help and support him and his siblings while they were there, and he seemed to remember every kindness, no matter how trivial. Even when he was our gray-haired Grandpa, he still remembered the Christmas when the Salvation Army brought each child in the orphanage a stuffed animal.

Remembering his stories motivates us to be that kindhearted person who makes a difference, however small, in someone's life, especially the children we meet in orphanages. We are often reminded

that we may be the first glimpse of Jesus anyone has seen. It's important to us to keep that in mind as we go about His work.

And it's another reason why we're so inspired to see the impact the
Benners, now in their eighties, have made in so many lives. Understanding that they've fed these children not only with food for their tummies
but also food for their spiritual lives is a powerful, living testimony that
shows what one person can do to make an *eternal* difference for others.

That lesson was also brought home in the Christian school we visited in El Salvador. Dad had been invited to speak to parents of the
students, so he shared his thoughts on the importance of raising children to have a ministry mind-set and a servant's heart, always looking
for ways to share God's love.

He expressed to the parents the needs that we had seen all around
them, practically in their own backyards, and how that was what
brought us back to their country time and again. At the end of Dad's
talk, he welcomed questions, and all of us participated in answering.
The questions continued for nearly ninety minutes. We were amazed
at how eager the parents were to know more about the work our team
was doing and how they could get involved.

Our family gathered at a local airport for a prayer and
encouragement-filled sendoff when our brother Joseph left for nine
weeks of Air Land Emergency Resource Team training.

Even after the program officially ended and we were making our way to the door, parents continue to reach out to us. For example, one mom asked me (Jessa) for ideas about how she could encourage her daughter regarding proper relationships with boys, and I was glad to step aside with her and share the guidelines we older Duggar girls have adopted for ourselves with the help of our parents.

Many of the families whose children attend the school are quite wealthy, and they pay a substantial tuition, which, in turn, pays the way for the poorer children who also attend. The main message our team hoped to impart during our time there was the urgent need for those Christians to reach out to others in their area, including the children in the orphanages, with the gospel message and the love of God.

The same goes for all of us. Wherever God has placed us, there are needs all around us. We pray that each one of us will be attentive to see the needs of others and take the opportunities God gives us to share the love of Jesus with others.

It is so neat to see how God works. We are praying that someday many of these El Salvador Christian school students may be the ones God uses to reap the seeds we have sown at the orphanage and guide someone into a relationship with our Savior. And also, in a future visit, maybe we will reap the seeds *they* sow.

We had come on this trip to help and encourage others, but on the last night of our trip, as with every trip, it was clear that *we* were the ones who'd gotten the biggest blessings, a reminder of Jesus's teaching that "it is more blessed to give than to receive." We were greatly blessed—especially as we considered the work of those who had devoted their whole lives to helping the people we had only briefly visited.

The Power of a Single Life

In addition to the Benners, who started the orphanage and school, our friends Mike Schadt and Alex Lara have also impacted many for

Christ. Mike is an ex-pro beach volleyball player who was radically saved. He and his wife, Sandy, became missionaries to Italy but had to come back to the States after his wife ended up with Lyme disease. After they returned, Mike prayed about how he could minister to those around him, and he got an idea to offer to teach English as a Second Language (ESL) classes at a local college in Clearwater, Florida.

Alex Lara was a young Salvadoran rural health worker who was awarded a scholarship to come to America for additional medical training. While he was attending medical-related courses in Clearwater, he also signed up for Mike's free English classes. Mike used the Spanish-English Bible as the textbook.

As Alex soaked up the English lessons, he also heard a clear gospel message and ended up committing his life to following Christ. Mike went on to share many Bible truths with Alex over the next few months, but then the time came for Alex to return to his own country. Mike told Alex to stay in touch and asked him to let him know if there was ever anything Mike could do for him.

After Alex returned to El Salvador he did just that. He called Mike and asked him to consider coming down to help the people in his country. Mike agreed and ended up bringing a small team to do ministry work. They organized a special presentation in the center of town and also went door-to-door sharing the gospel. The team fell in love with the people in El Salvador, but eventually they had to say good-bye and return to the States.

A major earthquake struck El Salvador one month later. Villages were destroyed by the quake itself or the resulting mudslides. Alex made another call to Mike, and Mike quickly organized some Christian friends who collected cash, food, clothes, and other much-needed items and headed back to El Salvador. They went to work in devastated villages, clearing debris, handing out clothes and personal items, and sharing food, along with the gospel message. Alex and the people who received help were grateful for the relief efforts.

During the past twelve years, about every four months Mike Schadt has taken a group of people to Central America to do ministry work. Every year around Christmastime the teams take gifts with them and hold Christmas parties in the poor villages for the children; they also take beans, rice, and other necessities to the needy families there. Alex is now a leader in the church, and his wife, Mida, leads the women and children's ministry.

Today, Mike and Alex's legacy is shown in the Christian churches they have started in El Salvador and Honduras and in the lives of the many people they have helped. By helping restore homes destroyed by natural disasters and by assisting the poverty-stricken residents in other ways, they have helped hearts of the villagers open up to the gospel, and many have received God's gift of salvation.

Mike's ministry in El Salvador eventually turned into SOS Ministries International (soshope.org), which now sends Christians who have a desire to serve on mission trips to impoverished areas in Africa, Asia, and the Americas to share the gospel while also helping with physical needs.

We joined Ray Comfort in sharing the gospel during our visit to Washington, D.C.

Again and again in their work they have seen what happens when a single heart is turned toward God. Just as Alex's faith eventually inspired his wife and other family members to believe, one person who becomes a Christian and dedicates his or her life to living for

God can have a powerful impact on his or her family. And that family, in turn, can impact dozens of others.

It's the same way Grandma Duggar, after becoming a Christian at age fifteen when no one else in her family believed, has had such a widespread influence as the years passed. She planted the love of God in the hearts of her children, who grew up to share that love with their own children. That would be *us!*

When we truly turn over the control of our lives to Jesus Christ, God's spirit then lives in us, and His love will overflow out of our lives through our words and deeds. Once we experience His love and forgiveness, we want to share it with others! And that relationship with *others* is what this chapter is about. The Bible tells us we are not supposed to express love only through our words but, even more important, through our actions as well, so *serving* others should be the primary focus of true Christians (see 1 John 3:18).

Jesus taught that we're to treat others as we want to be treated. And He also said we're to extend kindness to "strangers." He told His disciples a parable about a time when God will separate "His sheep from the goats"—in other words, the blessed from the cursed. Describing that time in the future, He said the blessed ones were those who had fed Him when He was hungry, gave Him a drink when He was thirsty, sheltered Him when He was a stranger, clothed Him when He was in need, looked after Him when He was ill, and visited Him when He was in prison.

In the parable, Jesus's followers were confused, thinking they hadn't done *any* of those things for Him. They asked, "Lord, when did we see you hungry?"

Jesus explained, "Inasmuch as ye have done it unto one of the least of these my brethren, ye have done it unto me" (Matthew 25:40).

Those words empower us to carry His love out into what Christians call "the mission field," whether it's "the least of these" in a family living in a mud hut in Honduras; a confused, hard-hearted girl living in an orphanage in El Salvador; or someone living closer to home.

Jesus's words also influence us Duggar girls in the way we've prepared for our adult years. We all hope to be wives and mothers someday, if that's in God's plan for us, so in the meantime we're preparing for marriage and motherhood by acquiring as many skills as possible. We believe one of the best preparations for marriage is to develop a selfless, giving mind-set that is always looking for ways to serve others, which is another way of serving the Lord.

Discovering Our Own Ministries

In considering ideas and opportunities for training, education, and ministry, our parents have been of great help; they've encouraged us to build on our strengths and talents, and not to fear stepping out into something new. We want to learn all we can and prepare to do work that gives us tools and brings opportunities to share God's love with others. That's the *career* we want in life.

In the rest of this chapter, we'll share how God has opened doors for us to let us see work we can do for Him—and where that work has taken us.

Volunteers in the Fire Department

After our brother John-David joined the local volunteer fire department, Jill and I (Jana) became interested in the work he was doing (and the adventures he was having!). So we joined, too. The three of us completed emergency response training and became Certified First Responders.

Our purpose in joining the department was to gain practical medical skills that would enable us to help the people in our community and in our own family. Since then, we've had hundreds of opportunities to assist in a variety of emergency situations, from car rollovers caused by drunk drivers to people having heart attacks. Sometimes in our small town we even get called out to things like a little old lady's cat stuck in a tree or a kid with his lip stuck in a sippie cup (true story!).

Even though Jill and I have been trained in how to put out fires, we'll probably stick to running the pumps on the fire trucks. Since there are plenty of guys in our volunteer department, we're not the ones going into burning buildings; we leave that to the men. At the same time, we know that a woman's presence—say, in the case of a woman in labor—is much appreciated!

In May 2011, our training led us to Joplin, Missouri, after the devastating F5 tornado destroyed parts of the city. Joplin is just a ninety-minute drive north of our home, so we gathered up equipment and supplies and headed up there within hours of the tornado hitting that area. As the sun rose over the city, we joined a special response team from Arkansas assigned to search the local Home Depot, which had been leveled by 189-mile-per-hour winds.

Jana also completed the emergency-response training and served with our volunteer fire department, but she's discontinued that work since her involvement with Journey to the Heart retreats takes her away from home.

The former building was nothing but a tangled mass of steel, concrete, shelving, merchandise, and other debris that had blown into the site. As our work began, we hoped to find survivors but knew it would be difficult to get them out of the wreckage without causing further injury. Several people had been shopping in the store as the clouds started to swirl late in the day on May 22. Several others were driving nearby and, realizing it was simply too dangerous to stay on the road, rushed into the huge store, seeking shelter from the storm.

One such driver was a dad with his two small children, an eighteen-month-old boy and a five-year-old girl. He called his wife to let her know they were hurrying into the Home Depot for safety. A worker inside the building was finding customers and rushing them to a safe room in the back. Suddenly, the tornado's fierce winds smashed into the store, knocking the thick exterior walls to the ground and caving in the roof from front to back. The worker who was rushing others to safety was among the dead found by Jill and John's team at the front of the building. He had been coming back to the storefront to help more people when the building collapsed. Many survived because he led them to the safe room, but he did not.

The search process grew increasingly grim as the work shifted from trying to be careful not to crush potential survivors to simply avoiding doing more damage to the bodies buried beneath the tons of rubble. The team pulled body after body from the wreckage, some of us holding up tarps to shield the scene from bystanders, many of whom were anxious family members hoping their loved ones had survived.

Workers cut chunks of concrete so we could pull the pieces off crushed victims. As one large chunk came up, we saw a man lying facedown. Over his shoulder we could see little fingers, and on the other side another little hand reached from beneath him. It was the man and his two young children.

We held it together as we plowed through the dreary day. There was too much to do to stop and think about how awful it was. But later on, during debriefing, the day's events began to sink in. So many lives were lost, so many families were ripped apart, so many hearts were broken; the grief threatened to overwhelm us. But at the same time we were thankful God had allowed us to receive emergency-response training years before, which enabled us to serve the people of Joplin in this very challenging situation.

Seeing such tragedies firsthand reminds us how important it is to always be available to help and to serve. It also emphasizes the value of life and of making wise use of each day because we don't know what tomorrow holds.

While our emergency and first responder work led Jill and me (Jana) into medical-related fields, it's not quite Jinger's and Jessa's thing. But after Josie was born prematurely, all four of us completed neonatal resuscitation training so we could help in that kind of scary situation, should it occur. (Seeing three-year-old Josie run around the house now like an energetic fireball, it's hard to remember the time our family prayed for every breath she took as a twenty-two-ounce preemie!)

Jill: Becoming a Midwife

My (Jill's) interest in midwifery may have been sparked when Mom welcomed us older girls to be with her and Dad during a couple of births. I considered many other types of work,

On December 15, 2009, the day after half of our family had returned from El Salvador, everyone drove to Little Rock to see their new baby sister, Josie Brooklyn Duggar.

too, but I prayed that God would show me His will and that He would make it so clear I wouldn't miss it. He has done that, and I'm so grateful!

Several years ago I did some babysitting for a doula, the professional name for a childbirth educator—someone who provides emotional support and guidance for parents as they go through the birthing process. I was interested in the work she did and loved hearing her talk about it, but I wasn't thinking of going into that field myself. I was still seeking the Lord's will for whatever skills He was leading me to.

And then, last year, a midwife/preceptor moved to our area; as a licensed midwife, she is qualified to deliver babies, usually in the local birthing center or in private homes, and as a preceptor, she's qualified to help train others in midwifery through apprenticeships. A friend of a friend introduced us, and after we had talked she offered me a chance to apprentice with her.

I prayed about the decision and talked to my parents. Then we prayed together (no big decisions are made without prayer in the Duggar family!), and they encouraged me to walk through these doors that God was opening for me.

Meanwhile, the midwife/preceptor I work with is fluent in Spanish and has many Spanish-speaking clients, so that's a big help in my efforts to become fluent in that language. Many people who hear about my apprenticeship assume that women in our area who choose home deliveries are Christian, homeschooling moms like my mom. But that's not the case. Most of our clients are not believers. And many of the birthing mothers I've helped have been single moms.

I've attended births in bright, clean, happy homes—and also in dingy, backwoods shacks where an abundance of curse words and alcohol seemed to be an ordinary part of the evening. No matter where it happens, the birth of a baby is an amazing thing, and I feel blessed to play a tiny part in bringing God's blessings into the world. I usually ask the mom if I can pray for her and her baby—especially when problems occur. The mom almost always says yes, and it is such a precious opportunity to be the first to pray a blessing over a newborn baby. Sometimes, when the mom is open to it, I also give the baby a gift—a little Bible.

Of all the births I've been a part of, our experience in China was probably the most memorable, and I wasn't even allowed to be in the delivery room for it, even though the parents wanted me to be there. Instead my role was limited to pacing and praying in the hallway.

It happened last year when our family traveled to China on ten-day journalism visas so we could record some episodes for the TV series. Our production coordinator, Courtney Enlow, wife of our videographer, Scott Enlow, was a little more than seven months pregnant at the time, but she'd gotten the go-ahead from her doctor to make the trip. We brought along an obstetrics nurse, just in case, and everything went well until, midway through our China visit, Courtney slipped and fell on some steps leading down to the subway from Tiananmen Square.

There didn't seem to be an immediate problem, but Courtney was a bit rattled and went back to the hotel to rest for a while. When she got up later that day to eat something, her water broke—which meant her baby was on its way! It also meant we were about to see a whole different side of the communist country we were visiting—one we would have preferred to miss.

To tell the entire story, with all its complexities and frustrations, we would need a separate book. In this limited space, I'll just tell you that, once again, God answered prayer and pushed aside a lot of otherwise impossible obstructions and regulations so that little Leah Enlow was successfully ushered into this world by a Chinese obstetrical team.

The actual birth itself was about the only "normal" part of the days surrounding her arrival, at least by American standards. When Courtney was hospitalized (China requires that all babies are born in hospitals), we were shocked to see less-than-ideal conditions there (including lots of black mold in the bathroom). At one point Scott stepped outside the hospital for a moment and saw a crowd of people peering into an open hospital window. He walked over to see what everyone was staring at and was surprised to find that they were watching a doctor operate on a patient's neck.

We were also stunned to learn that, in China, patients must supply their own linens and medical supplies. So Jana and I were constantly running back and forth to the store in the hospital basement buying bedsheets and towels, a bedpan and IV bags, diapers, and baby items!

Courtney was there overnight before Leah was born, and she went for long stretches of time when no one in the hospital even looked in on her. I was glad I could be there most of the time early on in her labor to check her progress, encourage her, and help her get into some

It's hard to imagine now that the little girl playing dress-up with Josiah would one day be helping with deliveries (Jana is on the far right).

positions that would ease her discomfort. When the doctor announced that the baby was on its way, Scott and I helped push Courtney's bed to the other side of the (huge) hospital. Then we were told to wait in the hallway.

Scott protested that he was the dad and he *had* to be there, and Courtney was saying the same thing. The idea seemed entirely foreign to the Chinese team, but they reluctantly agreed to let him come in after he had scrubbed up. They said they would come and get him when they had prepped Courtney to push. But they forgot about him! And once again, he had to insist that they let him in. They said okay, but there was no way they were letting me into the delivery room, too. Courtney said that when they rolled her into the delivery room, the last baby that was born (a little girl) was still lying on a table, still covered in blood and mucus. The newborn lay there crying the whole time, unattended, while Courtney was delivering Leah.

Courtney had expected to have an epidural to ease the pain of delivery, but during the hospital admitting process she was told that the hospital didn't keep epidurals in stock and that mothers had to order them at the beginning of their pregnancies! So she was heading into delivery without the pain medication she'd hoped for—while all the Duggars and production team members prayed that her labor would be short, that the delivery would be problem-free, and that the hospital staff would show mercy to this worried mom-to-be. And that's what happened. The beautiful Leah Adee Enlow arrived safely, and her parents were allowed a quick peek at her.

Then the hospital staff instantly hustled Leah away to the nursery, where parents were not allowed. They told the Enlows they could see Leah in three days. *Three days!* There wasn't even a window in the nursery so parents and visitors could see the babies. Apparently the staff claimed that the no-visitors, no-viewing rule was to protect the babies from outside germs. And maybe that would have been halfway believable except that one day when Scott was there, begging to see his daughter, a small motorcycle drove down the hospital corridor, apparently making deliveries of mail or supplies!

At one point staffers told Scott he could see the baby if he paid three hundred dollars. He paid. And they said, "Sorry. It'll be awhile longer. The baby still needs some more tests."

The excuses of mysterious and unnamed "tests" stretched on and on, and all of us were on edge, knowing this kind of separation wasn't good for the baby or her parents. The other issue was that our ten-day visas were about to expire, and all of us, even the Enlows, would have no choice but to leave the country—or be threatened with arrest.

Still the hospital staff hesitated. They told Scott and Courtney they could go to Hong Kong and reapply for visas and then come back for their baby. It all seemed too bizarre to understand. We spent our last few days in China in lots of prayer and mainly just trying to console and encourage Scott and Courtney.

Finally, the American ambassador to China got involved, and on the day before our visas expired, the tests were "magically" completed, and little Leah was allowed to leave the hospital—and the country. I don't think any of us had ever been so relieved to head home as we were that day when we all finally boarded the plane, sending up prayer

When we boarded the plane to come home from China, our group of family and film crew had one more member than when we arrived. Leah Enlow, daughter of our production coordinator, Courtney Enlow, and her husband, videographer Scott Enlow, was born (prematurely) while we were there.

after prayer of thankfulness that God had seen us through this trying time.

The experience was scary, exhausting, and also very confirming, showing us again how much we need to rely on God as He leads us through situations that might seem intolerable or even impossible at first. It also confirmed for me that midwifery is work I can use to serve Him wherever I am. Now I'm looking forward to completing my national certification so I can continue to serve God in this way for as long as He chooses to keep this pathway open for me.

Jana: Journey to the Heart

Jill and I (Jana) love sharing in the birthing process, and we've both found a way to be involved. While I've had quite a bit of midwife training, I feel called to focus on childbirth coaching and prenatal preparation instead of "running the show," as Jill does so competently when she serves as midwife. I love helping the mom- or parents-to-be get ready for the birth by coaching them through breathing and stretching exercises; it's a joy to see them approach the birth with a sense of happy anticipation rather than nervous anxiety. Helping expectant parents know what to expect can give them a greater sense of peace and well-being when the contractions begin, and it's very rewarding to see that happen. The other thing I really enjoy is working with Jill as a team during a birth. It's a blessing to see her working with her calm, confident skill to help bring another baby into the world.

But during the last year or so God has also opened a door for me to serve in a ministry called Journey to the Heart. I've stepped back from my work as a first responder and as a birthing coach because my work with Journey usually requires quite a bit of my time.

Journey is a program for young people—teenagers and young adults, plus a new program designed for moms—offered by the Institute in Basic Life Principles (IBLP). It can be presented in different settings and for different lengths of time; in fact, most recently, Jessa, Jinger, and I worked as leaders and assistants in a seven-day Journey to the Heart seminar in a high-security prison in Florida (Jinger will tell you more about that later). Most of the Journeys are ten-day retreats where attendees gather at the IBLP headquarters in Chicago for a couple of days of preparation before traveling to the beautiful Northwoods Conference Center in Michigan. This is where the "real work" is done as the larger groups of ten-person teams break into individual times where it's just you and God.

Over the years we Duggar kids have chosen not to attend youth camps and the like because we prefer to attend conferences together as a family. But we have also seen the importance of this Journey to the Heart for each one of us older children, setting aside a week where it's just us and God. No distractions with cell phones, computers, or the daily routines back home. At Journey, you get down into the deep issues of the heart, and ask God to search you and try you, and determine what areas of your life are hindering you from having a close relationship with Him.

We Duggar girls had our first experience with Journey to the Heart in 2009, and we were blessed to have our sister-in-law Anna's sister Priscilla as our leader. Journey leads participants to study eighteen "heart conditions" described in the Bible, both good conditions (like a pure heart, humble heart, or forgiving heart, for example) and bad conditions (for example, a "murmuring heart" focused on negativity and complaining). This journey helps participants focus on getting their heart "right" with the Lord and understanding His heart's desire for them. In addition, powerful video messages and testimonies help attendees understand who God is, and they learn how to trust Him more fully. As a Journey leader, I get to see God working in the hearts of these individuals, and there's just no experience like it.

The girls I've worked with in Journey to the Heart come from *very* diverse backgrounds. Some come from homeschool families. Some have been to church a few times but don't have a clear perspective of who Jesus is. Some participants come from a very rough background; they may have been involved in drugs or crime of some sort, and their parents have sent them to Journey as a last resort, hoping their daughter can be "fixed." At one Journey retreat this year, I was amazed to learn that several participants had come from Korea, Israel, and Singapore.

Sometimes I don't know the girls' backgrounds, but as we get to know each other over the ten days we spend together, they start opening up and sharing more about themselves. We try to have one-on-one conversations whenever the girls are ready for that step. In almost every retreat there are girls who don't want to be there, but again and again I've seen how God can soften their hearts and open their minds so that by the end of the retreat they seem like different people. It's not at all unusual to have these girls reluctantly tell us on the last day, "I don't want to leave!"

A lot of these girls have never had somebody sit down and ask them the hard questions—like, What are you going through right now? What's the deepest hurt in your life?—and then listen to their answers, help them sort out their feelings, and consider what next steps would be most likely to bring healing to the hurts they've experienced.

I've been amazed to hear girl after girl express heartache about her relationship with her father. When I think back on the girls I've worked with, I estimate that more than half have been emotionally hurt by their dad.

Again and again girls talk about their dad's anger in the home and how badly their dad's angry words have hurt their young and tender hearts. One girl said her dad was like a volcano when he erupted in anger. And she added, "Even if a volcano only erupts once a year, no one wants to live close to it."

We pray for special blessings on those girls, asking that God would give them peace, that He would shield their hearts from the angry words, and help them respond in a calm manner. As God tells us, "A soft answer turneth away wrath, but grievous words stir up anger" (Proverbs 15:1). And we also join those girls in prayer for their dads, asking God to replace their negative characteristics with positive ones. That in place of anger, God would give those dads peace; in place of frustration, patience.

At the end of most Journeys, we have a wonderful time of blessing. We usually suggest that each girl call her dad or mom and ask if one or both of them will call back at a certain time the next day and pray a blessing over their daughter. Some of these girls don't come from Christian homes, and in that case, if they are uncomfortable with this, we ask church leaders to pray a special blessing.

One young teenager who did come from a Christian family had struggled through lots of secrets and heartache during the retreat, and God had worked a miraculous change in her heart. She had called home and told her parents what she had been struggling with for the past several years, and they were able to work through a lot of her problems. As we neared the end of the retreat, she realized there were many things she needed to give up, and as she gave God control of these areas, she was happy about the changes He was making in her life. But then she came to me with the saddest look on her face.

When I asked gently, "How are you doing?" she started bawling.

She had excitedly called home and said, "Dad, they're going to have a prayer time for dads and moms to pray a blessing for their daughters. It's tomorrow morning at ten o'clock. Could you call then and pray over me?"

My heart broke for her when she said, "My dad said he doesn't want to."

I didn't know what to say, so I just gave her a hug. "He didn't say,

'I don't want to pray for you,'" she said between sobs. "He was, like, 'I don't know about that. I don't know if I'd feel comfortable doing that. I'd rather not.'"

The father's words deeply hurt this girl, who was probably thirteen or fourteen. Some of the other participants and leaders gathered around her and prayed with her. Something discussed a lot during Journey is how God can use difficult situations to grow us and make us stronger. After her tears were dried, one of the leaders said, "You know, we're going to face lots of trials in life, and we can respond the wrong way by holding the hurt inside and getting bitter—but that will only hurt us more in the long run. Or we can choose to forgive and then pray that God will bless the person who hurt us with the character quality that person is lacking. In your dad's case, that would be sensitivity. When we're in the middle of tough situations like this, we have two choices: we can either become bitter, or better."

We also told her that many other fathers and pastors would be happy to pray over her. I suggested that she read her Bible and think about some of the things we'd talked about during the retreat and that she look for Scripture verses she could pray for her dad.

The girl left the room, and about an hour later, as we were talking to another girl, she burst in and said, "Girls! I'm so excited! I found these verses, and it's so perfect for what I'm working through right now."

She had found scriptures promising that, no matter what happens, no matter who else turns away from us, God will not forsake us.

"I think you're right," the girl said. "This is a testing for me, showing me that God wants me to treasure His love even more than anyone else's." And then she added, "I prayed for Dad. And, really, I think it's probably a misunderstanding."

The next day came, and her dad didn't call. But by that point, the girl was so assured of God's love for her that she could forgive her dad for his inability to respond the way she had desired him to.

Jinger: Ministering Behind Bars

Like Jana, Jill, and Jessa, I (Jinger) am at a time when I'm asking God to lead me in the direction He would have for my life. Photography is something I have enjoyed for several years now, and I'm constantly looking for ways I can use what I've learned, hoping it can be a blessing to others. Scott Enlow, the videographer for the *19 Kids and Counting* TV series, has been very kind to share his wealth of information and teach some of us kids about the technical side of photography as well as sharing tips on things like composition and framing. I was honored to be asked to take individual portraits and family photos for some political candidates during the last campaign season, and I love snapping photos of our family whenever we're traveling.

A friend and I also photographed a wedding—a rather scary thing for us because neither of us had done a wedding before. One concern was the lighting. We were hoping we wouldn't have to use flash, both

We are humbled to be invited to play our violins (and, in Josiah's case, the cello) at places such as Charles Stanley's church, where this photo was taken.

because the pictures aren't as pretty and also because the flash itself would distract from the ceremony. We did a lot of preparation and praying in the days leading up to the wedding, and God helped us stay calm and focused (literally!) on the job at hand. When it was all said and done, the couple was pleased with the way the pictures turned out, and we were thankful for that.

One area of ministry I've felt a calling for is the juvenile detention center in our area. Every other week I go there with a couple of other ladies and usually one or two of my sisters to minister to girls who are in lockup there.

The kids at the detention center are eleven to seventeen, and they're usually in "juvy" because they stole something, or maybe they've been caught with drugs, or somehow they just ended up in the wrong place at the wrong time with the wrong people. Most are there for a relatively short time, no more than a month or two, but occasionally we talk to a teenager who's done something violent and is facing serious consequences.

So many times we find that these kids are at the end of themselves. They feel lost and broken, and they're looking for help, searching for answers in life. Looking for a way out of the downward spiral they seem to have fallen into, they are often receptive and sometimes even *eager* to hear what we have to say. Often we can tell that God has gone before us and softened the heart of at least one young girl who acknowledges her need for true repentance and God's forgiveness and wants to trust Christ as Savior.

So many times in ministry, you reach out to someone with your testimony or some other information about the gospel, and that person just isn't interested. But in juvy, more times than not, the teens we talk to are ready to listen.

We pray with them and talk to them about what it means to be free in Christ. Sometimes we meet with a girl who's terribly sad and close to despair. She thinks no one could ever forgive her for what she's done and that this is the way her life is going to be from now on. But we are able to tell her about God, who loves her no matter what, and who can forgive *everything*. To see a girl light up when she understands and accepts this truth is very exciting.

I've been so blessed by this work, which was motivated largely by my time at the Journey to the Heart retreat with my sisters back in 2009. So you might think that when I was invited to help with a Journey to the Heart program at a women's prison in Florida, I would see it as the perfect way to combine two of my favorite ministries.

Not!

I felt scared, not about being in the prison, but I was afraid I was too young and wouldn't know what to say to women who could be the age of my mother—or grandmother!

I sought advice from my mom. "Why are they asking *me* to go? I don't know what I would say to older people. I'm used to working with kids."

Mom told me, "Jinger, this is not about *you*. It's about Jesus and sharing His love. When the time comes, God will put on your heart what He wants you to share with these ladies."

So I prayed and read my Bible. I was inspired by 1 Timothy 4:12: "Let no man despise thy youth; but be thou an example of the believers, in word, in conversation, in charity, in spirit, in faith, in purity." Even though I am young, I desired to be an example of believers!

At that point it was easier to say, "Okay, Lord. I had the wrong perspective. I understand now: it's about *You*."

About forty of us, both men and women, gathered in Florida for that Journey to the Heart. We stayed at a camp a few miles from the prisons and slept in bunkhouses, one for the women, one for the men. Every morning for seven days, we woke up about 5 A.M. (a stretch for us night-owl Duggars!) to get ready and then make the thirty-minute drive to the prison complex, arriving about 7 A.M. The men headed to the men's prison and the women to the women's. We passed through airport-type security and finally met the Journey participants.

As we entered the room, we received a special welcome from the ladies who had gathered; all were very eager to learn more about God. The lines of grief and bitterness could be seen on many of their faces as a result of the poor decisions that had led up to their incarceration. We prayed that God would use us to bring to every one of these women the hope and healing that we ourselves have found in His forgiveness.

As we began to greet the ladies one by one and looked deep into their eyes, we remembered Dad's words to us growing up: God sees everyone the same. We are all sinners. So we can never compare ourselves to others and think that we are somehow better than they are.

He would also tell us that a person doesn't just wake up one day and decide, *Hey, nice day for robbing a bank. I think that's what I'll do today*. It starts with one small, bad decision that leads to a bigger bad decision, and before you know it you've done something you never saw yourself capable of doing. As the saying goes, "Sin will take you farther than you want to go, keep you longer than you want to stay, and cost you more than you want to pay."

Classic hymns of the Christian faith are taught in our home from an early age. Here you see Jessa leading in song around our family table.

Our hearts were full of compassion and love for those women. Each morning we started with the large-group meeting. Being that this was our first time in a prison, all of us girls were struck by the world in which these women live. Massive fences are topped with three rows of barbed wire, and a center guard tower controls all doors and gates. About a hundred women had signed up for Journey. As a prerequisite, a few months prior, all of them had completed another IBLP program called the Basic Seminar, a sort of introduction to Christian living.

Each morning during Journey, the group heard a video message followed by personal testimonies from some of the leaders or assistants, who talked about things like former addictions or fears. Next we worked through the Journey to the Heart material assigned for that day.

Then came a break when each person "got alone with the Lord," as we described it, to ask Him to reveal the negative heart conditions or other areas each woman needed to work on. Each one was given a Journey binder that included journal pages where she could record her prayers as well as the direction in which she felt God leading her.

Jana was serving as a small-group leader, and Jessa and I came along as assistant leaders, but the leader I was assisting was the organizer of the complete women's Journey team, and she often had to step away to help another leader or speak to prison officials, so I was often left in charge of leading the team time for my group. "My" ladies ranged in age from twenty-three to sixty-five—definitely different from the juvenile detention center, where the oldest person I'd worked with was seventeen!

One of the major differences between Journey seminars held in a quiet retreat or in a prison was that, at any moment, a session in the prison could be interrupted by a "call-out," when a prison guard would step into the room where we were meeting and call out the names of inmates who had to leave for various reasons. Usually after the large-group session we would split up into our small groups of ten to twelve women, but one day so many women were called out that only two women were left in my small group. But the amazing thing was that the Lord knew exactly who needed to be there. The two women who were left that day were from the same dorm and had held hard grudges against each other for quite some time. In that quiet, very personal setting, they were able to make things right and apologize to one another for their wrong attitudes and actions.

Working seven days straight in the prison from 8 A.M. to 8 P.M., I expected to be exhausted. And I'll admit, at the end of the first day, I was pretty tired. But after that, I felt energized because while God was working on the hearts of the inmates we were serving, He was also doing an amazing work within our own hearts and strengthening us too! It was sometimes overwhelming to see how He continually worked to open these ladies' hearts and minds to His love and grace.

Sometimes this happened through the simplest comments. For example, on the first days we were there, one of the women in my group who had a daughter my age asked if we were going to the beach after Journey ended. She assumed that, coming from a landlocked state like Arkansas at the end of winter, we would want to enjoy a spring break trip to soak up some sunshine on Florida's beautiful shoreline.

No, we told her, no beach trips are planned.

Oh, she said, eyebrows raised.

Then she said she'd heard there were some good antiques shops in the area, and she asked if we had found time to go shopping.

No, we told her, no shopping, either. "We're only here because we wanted to bring God's love to you," we said. "You're the only reason we've come."

The thought seemed almost shocking to some of the participants overhearing the conversation, and it obviously carried a heartfelt message: that they mattered more to us than a Florida vacation. And equally surprising to them was that the Journey team members spent the whole day in the prisons. They told us that other volunteers who had come in would usually leave to eat lunch in town somewhere. But most days, we ate both lunch and supper with the inmates, sitting with them at the stainless-steel tables in the huge dining hall and eating exactly what they ate.

Sure, we probably could have gotten tastier food in a nearby restaurant, and the dining experience would have been quieter and less stressful. (At least once during each meal, and sometimes two or three times, prison guards would call out, "Count!" which indicated that all volunteers were required to stand at the table—or sometimes against a wall—so that all the inmates could be counted to ensure no one was missing.) But what amazing opportunities we would have missed if we hadn't shared those meals with the women we were serving!

However, for me, it wasn't the meal itself that led to the most life-changing moments but the simple walk to and from the dining hall. The various prison dormitories are connected to the dining hall by eight-foot-wide sidewalks, each painted with yellow lines two feet from the edges. The inmates are required to walk within those outer borders so there's no opportunity for contact with inmates who might be walking in the other direction along the opposite edge. Only volunteers and prison guards and officials are allowed to walk in the center of the sidewalk. Most of the time, we walked in line with the inmates, but sometimes being able to walk alongside one of the women provided the opportunity for a brief, heart-to-heart talk.

These talks were powered by prayer and scripted by God. Each day as we rode to and from the prisons in large vans, and also during each day's late-afternoon gathering of the entire Journey team, we would share prayer requests for the inmates we were working with, and we would also share scriptures that could be helpful for an individual. We watched in awe as so many hearts were turned. It was a week of miracle after miracle as God worked wonders within the inmates we were serving.

For example, one of the inmates I was working with was probably in her mid-thirties. I'd been praying for her, and I'd asked the other team members for guidance in how to handle the questions she was raising and the attitude that seemed to be blocking her from being willing to give up everything for Jesus. One day as we walked to lunch, I asked her, "Are you a fan of Jesus or a follower? Are you just saying, 'Yay, Jesus!' or are you willing to lay down everything for Him?"

Some people love to stand in church on Sunday and sing all the songs, but they don't want God to interfere with the rest of their week. They are delighted with the thought of Jesus being our Savior, which literally means that He forgives our sins and saves us from judgment and spending eternity in hell. But they're not willing to give Him the place of Lord and Master, which means giving Him authority over and control of their daily life and allowing Him to remove anything from their lives that He doesn't approve of. But what they don't realize is that they can't have one without the other. If Jesus is your Savior, He also takes the position of your Lord and Master.

This woman obviously did a lot of thinking as she ate because as we left the dining hall that day she said, "Jinger, I think I'm ready to commit my life to the Lord."

We were all lined up on the yellow line, waiting to walk back to the meeting room. I was excited for her but didn't want to do anything that would get her in trouble with the guards. I said, "Do you want to wait until we get back to the room, or do you want to do it now?"

"Now!" she said excitedly. We quietly stepped onto the grass alongside the sidewalk and prayed together. And right there in the open, she committed her life to the Lord. What a moment! I almost felt that I heard the angels singing, right there inside the prison walls.

Another woman in my group seemed so wise with head knowledge of the Bible and Christianity, but when we talked about a personal relationship with Jesus she seemed to hold back. Much of the time she was there physically, but she was zoned out emotionally. She was in her mid-forties; she had only been in the prison a few months and seemed to be in denial about her situation. I kept thinking, *Something is different about her. But what is it?*

I asked the other team members to pray for her, and I prayed, too, that God would do whatever was necessary to bring her into the personal relationship with Him that she so needed.

The next morning when the session began, I asked the woman, "How are you doing today?"

"I'm doing great," she answered with a tight smile.

We continued with the day's schedule, and then a little later during a break I asked her again, "How are you doing?"

"Do you want to sit down?" she said.

I pulled two chairs together, and we sat. Immediately the tears started flowing as she shared some of what had been holding her back. She asked if I could walk to lunch with her, and she continued sharing as we walked. She asked questions about how she could have a real relationship with the Lord and what that would mean. And then, right there in front of everyone, she prayed in humility and repentance for God's Salvation. She asked Jesus to come into her life, and again the angels were surely rejoicing!

When I shared her story with the other leaders that evening, one of them commented, "That just goes to show that intellectually, a person can have all the head knowledge of the Bible and Christianity, but sometimes people stop short of truly knowing Jesus."

When this Journey experience began, the team leader told us she had a list of the participants and the crimes they'd been convicted of that led to their imprisonment. Most of us didn't want to know about the convictions going into the retreat because we knew that might subconsciously influence our work with the women. But as this woman shared her story with me, she told me she expected to spend the rest of her life behind bars. It turned out she'd been convicted of first-degree murder.

As we flew home from Florida at the end of our week in the prison, I thanked God for the time I'd been able to spend with each of those precious ladies.

When we were in El Salvador, working in the orphanages and making home visits in the remote villages, I had thought, *It just can't get any better than this. It's the most rewarding work anyone could hope for.* And then I spent that week working in the prison and realized that each new opportunity is more inspiring and energizing than the last. I can't wait to see what doors and new opportunities God will open in the future. As Dad says often, "Life is an exciting adventure when you're seeking to follow God!"

Jessa: By the Numbers

Like my siblings, I (Jessa) am grateful for the opportunities God provides for us to minister to others. For example, although I'm not nearly as skilled in photography as Jinger is, I've learned some things from her and from Scott, the family's videographer. When Jill came home from a day of midwife training and mentioned that some of her clients were wishing someone could photograph their baby's birth and precious first hours with parents, grandparents, and older siblings, the obvious choice was Jinger, the "family photog." But then we remembered that Jinger would probably pass out at the first sight of blood (proving again that all of us Duggars have our own personal likes, dislikes, abilities, and hang-ups).

So I offered to take on that job, and now I enjoy going along with Jill when her clients ask for childbirth videos and baby photos. When I get home, I edit the pictures and burn them onto a CD for the new parents to enjoy. Recording these happy events feels like another way we can help advocate what God says about children—that they are a blessing from Him.

Our parents have encouraged us to recognize, appreciate, and cultivate the gifts God has given us. It's been exciting to see what those unique gifts turn out to be. They are really a special feature designed by God as part of our unique makeup that prepares us for the special assignments He lays before us.

For instance, I really have a love for organizing things—and with a family the size of ours, God has given me *lots* of opportunities to put that skill to use. There's just something very satisfying about turning a big mess of clothes, shoes, papers and files, boxes, toys, and just about anything else into an orderly system. (I'm always a bit surprised when other people don't feel as excited as I do about being confronted with messy stacks, piles, and closets!)

Mom laughs when she tells about noticing that, as a child, I was always sorting our toys or rearranging things in the girls' room so that "like things" were together and constantly trying to coax my siblings into being neater. When she thought about it, she realized that when she was pregnant with me, she and Daddy were in the process of mov-

Our film crew has taught us a lot about photography, and they're patient when we want to take a peek through the lens.

ing our family from one house to another, and she read Emily Barnes's books on organizing and, as she puts it, "became gung-ho about organizing everything." Following Emily Barnes's suggestions, Mama put things in boxes, recorded each box's contents on an index card, numbered each box and card correspondingly, and developed a great system that she still uses today, all these years later.

Mama jokes that some of that clutter-busting creativity must've soaked into me as she was sorting and organizing because today, it's my thing. For years now, Jinger and I have worked together to pack for the younger kids whenever we're traveling; we've developed our own system, which has evolved over the years as the family has grown—and as individual family members have grown.

Joseph, Josiah, Jedidiah, and Jeremiah still appreciate it when we help them put together outfits and pack their clothes for them. We like to joke that we are their personal stylists! When they were little guys, we used to be able to fold all their shirts for one day and fit them in a single plastic grocery bag, with all their pants in another—it made it very easy each morning to grab just two bags and have everyone's clothes for the day.

Now that they're older and no longer "little kids," their larger-size clothes won't fit in those bags, but the idea remains the same. We fold and stack a day's worth of clothes for each of the kids and put them all into one large suitcase and label it just as we did when we used the plastic bag system, "Sunday, Monday, Tuesday . . ." Mornings on the road or in a hotel are simplified when we pack this way because all we need to do is grab one big suitcase, and all the kids have their preselected outfits for the day. On the packing side of things, it may take a little more effort at home before the trip to get everything preplanned and lined out like this, but in the long run, we save time and effort during the trip by not having to pull out fourteen different suitcases every morning.

In addition to being our younger brothers' "personal stylists," Jinger and I do hair, too. From the time we were young, Mom assumed the role of basic hair beautician, a skill she learned from her older sister, who did it professionally. With nineteen kids, this has saved our family thousands of dollars over the years, and since it's something she has passed on to us kids, it has the potential to keep saving us thousands more.

Recently, I've enjoyed watching how-to videos and experimenting on the guys with different haircuts. They are good to sit there for half an hour, if they have to, while I try to perfect a new cut. I guess if I make a mistake it wouldn't be too bad because a lot of them would prefer to have it all buzzed off anyway, but Jinger and I agree they should keep at least enough hair to style! And so far, they still listen to their "stylists."

Something else I enjoyed trying my hand at was helping to organize my younger siblings' daily schedule—from chores to schoolwork. Most of us have assisted Mom at one time or another with some one-on-one tutoring or grading papers, but some of us older Duggars find teaching to be our "thing," and we enjoy it more than the others do. I enjoy it because I love reading and studying and encouraging others to branch out and learn new things as well. Helping with homeschool

All of our trips take a lot of organizing! This trip out west took us to the spectacular Garden of the Gods near Colorado Springs, Colorado.

also taught me patience and creativity with the many different learning styles of my younger brothers and sisters.

Supervising the little ones' homeschool work also opened another opportunity for me. About four years ago, when I was helping Jackson and Johannah with their phonics and beginner math lessons, there would usually be a one-hour period each day when they were finishing assignments in their workbooks, and I would try to be nearby to answer questions (and also to make sure they didn't run off!). Our family loves music, and we all play classical piano and violin.

But occasionally one (or more) of us will branch out and try something new. That's how Jana, Jill, and Jinger developed their harp-playing skills. It's also how we expanded what we play so that now we enjoy traditional music as well as classical. That shift led our younger sister Joy-Anna to learn to play the violin "fiddle style." John took up the mandolin, and that prompted me to pick up the guitar. During those school times when Jackson and Johannah were working on math problems, I would grab the guitar and look up YouTube videos on a laptop computer to learn the basic chords. And whenever guitar-playing guests visited our family, I would ask them to show me different chords and techniques. That's one of the best ways to learn.

Music is another way our family ministers together. We are grateful for our music teachers (Ruth Anita Anderson and Mandy Query), who have spent many hours over the years teaching us to read notes and also to play by ear. But sometimes we still feel a little apprehensive when we're asked to play somewhere, whether it's for a church gathering, a program at the mall, a nursing home opportunity, a campaign appearance, or some other venue. But then we realize it's not about promoting ourselves, because there are tons of other people who play better than us! Our goal in playing music together is to show family unity and ultimately point people back to the source of that: God.

There's one other kind of training I'm working on now, and it's something I've enjoyed but wouldn't have thought of without my parents' suggesting it. Knowing how I like to keep things neat and tidy, they suggested I consider taking a bookkeeping course, so I added another life skill to my "toolbox," as Dad calls it. My brother Josiah also enrolled in the course because he loves math and numbers, and it's been good training for us both. Since then, we've been able to get some hands-on practice by helping keep the books for our family's commercial real estate business.

INTERACTING WITH THE WORLD — DUGGAR STYLE

IN THIS CHAPTER WE'VE shared how we cultivate new skills and use the talents and abilities God has given us to bless others. You can be sure He's blessed you with many gifts, too. We pray that you'll discover them, cherish them, and use them in ways that glorify Him wherever you go.

Before we move on, we'd like to share just a few other ideas our parents have instilled in us that help us show respect as we relate to the people around us—to strangers, new acquaintances, and old friends.

Here's Jana playing the harp that was given to her by a friend, Nana Paula.

Respect and Courtesy

Our parents would be the first to say they did not come up with all these child-rearing principles on their own. Most of these ideas for how we Duggars relate to others come from practices Mom picked up while watching families she respected. Whenever she would meet a family with older or grown kids who turned out well—especially families whose kids didn't go through a stage of rebellion—she would ask a lot of questions. She was never afraid to ask, and she's always sincere in wanting to know because she understands that a child's future depends largely on the foundations laid and principles taught to them when they were young.

Cultivating good manners is something that takes time and effort, probably more so on our parents' part than even our own. The goals we are listing here are just that, goals. And we don't have them down pat, but we're working toward them, especially with our younger siblings. We are so grateful for the many families and individuals who have shared practical tips with our family, and have encouraged us and blessed our lives over the years. That's what we hope to pass on to you by sharing these ideas.

For a moment, let's jump back almost thirty years and discuss the early days and the "how" and "why" behind Mom and Dad's decision to homeschool us kids. They had only been married for a few years when they first met a homeschooling family. Our parents were immediately struck by the good behavior the children demonstrated and by how well-rounded they were, easily interacting with adults as well as their peers.

It was then that they first began to contemplate the idea of one day homeschooling their own sons and daughters. Then they read the passage in Deuteronomy 6 that says it is the responsibility of parents to lead their children to love God with all their heart, soul, mind, and strength: "And these words, which I command thee shall be in thine heart: And thou shalt teach them diligently unto thy children, and shalt talk of them when thou sittest in thine house, and when thou walkest by the way, and when thou liest down, and when thou risest up." That passage solidified their decision to be the ones instructing their children, teaching them character and the ways of the Lord.

One of their main goals in homeschooling was to teach us respect: respect for God, respect for authorities, and respect for others' possessions. Mom and Dad have made good manners a priority in our family because this is one of the greatest ways to show respect for others.

Mom thoughtfully uses positive reinforcement to teach good manners. One thing she has practiced with all of us children at one time or another has been the "Yes, ma'am/Yes, sir" chart, which she posts on the kitchen wall. Mom taught us that we should respond with "Yes, ma'am" when she asks us to do something so that she knows we understand her and so there is no guessing as to whether we heard what she said. This is also a way to remind the younger children not to use "Uh-huh" or "Yeah." Each time they address an adult properly, they get a check mark. Once they get to a certain number of check marks, they earn a special reward.

Whether we're at one of our favorite spots in Branson, Missouri, or greeting a visitor at our home, we all practice being "enthusiastic."

Mom also addressed the issue of "I want . . ." or "I never got . . ." and began giving check marks for asking, "May I please . . . ?"

Gratefulness is one of the most important character qualities a parent can instill in the lives of their children, and it is vital to do it while they are young. Mom taught us the power behind the two simple words *thank you*. I (Jessa) remember us going to a family's house for supper one evening when I was eight years old, and before we piled out of the van, Mom reminded us kids, "I want every one of you individually to tell Mr. and Mrs. Bell, 'Thank you for having us in your home this evening,' or 'Thank you for supper. It was delicious!'" She went on to say, "When we get back in the car to leave, I hope each one of you will have expressed gratefulness to their family."

Those who said "Thank you" were able to put a check mark on their manners chart when we got home.

Several years ago we added "my pleasure" to the manners chart after we read the book *How Did You Do It, Truett?* by S. Truett Cathy, founder of Chick-fil-A. In it, Mr. Cathy tells how he studied the methods of five-star hotels and found that workers are required to say "My pleasure" instead of "You're welcome" when being thanked for something. In essence, one is saying, "Thank you for giving me the pleasure of serving you," and not, "Yes, it was such a sacrifice on my part. You're welcome."

He found a direct link between business success and employees learning to treat costumers with the utmost courtesy and respect, and that was one of the principles he adopted for all Chick-fil-A workers.

An Enthusiastic Greeting

Years ago at the Advanced Training Institute family conference we attend every year, our parents heard a testimony about the benefits of learning how to give an enthusiastic, friendly greeting to others. When we returned home from the conference, Mom lined us up from oldest to youngest and she explained the importance of each one of us developing these new communication skills.

This greeting rehearsal occurred when Joy-Anna (now sixteen) was the youngest in the family. She was barely able to understand what was going on, but Mom had all of us practice our "enthusiastic greetings."

"Okay, I'll go down the line, and everybody is going to give it a try," Mom told us. "I'll pretend I'm someone you're meeting for the first time. You need to have a big smile on your face, and when that person comes up to you, stick your hand out, give a firm handshake, say, 'Hello,' and then say your name and 'It's very nice to meet you.'" Josh, the oldest, went first. Then Jana, John-David, Jill, Jessa, Jinger, Joseph, Josiah, and finally Joy-Anna. When it was Joy-Anna's turn, she confidently stepped up and in rapid-fire robotic words said, "HellomynameisJoyAnnait'sverynicetomeetyou." The words ran together and had us all chuckling. Mom gave the little girl credit for trying and encouraged her to slow down next time. *Way* down. And enunciate carefully and give a firm handshake.

Back to the top again with Josh. Again, the process went smoothly, and child after child came to the front of the line and followed the instructions perfectly. Then Joy-Anna stepped up. As though stuck in slow motion, she began, "Hellllooo. My . . . name . . . is . . ." Before she could finish, the room burst out in laughter, Joy included. When you're a toddler, it's hard to get things just right.

Greeting people doesn't come naturally to most little kids, especially when they're greeting someone they don't know. Especially adults they don't know. Their natural tendency is to turn away, and many parents understandably explain, "He's shy."

Mom has not allowed us to get away with that—although we all tried it at some point. In every case, Mom and Dad made it crystal clear that turning away is unacceptable when we're greeting someone, even if we're uncomfortable facing the person. Most of us only tried not responding *once*.

Our parents understand that there are different personality

types—that some of us like to talk more and others less. They're not trying to conform us all to the same mold. But they encourage each of us individually to look beyond ourselves and think about others. Instead of thinking about our own comfort, we're encouraged to look for ways to make the *other* person feel more comfortable and relaxed.

Dad always reminds us, "Even if you stereotype yourself as an 'introvert' or if you just don't feel like saying anything, others may take that as rejection or assume you're a snob with a *I'm too good to talk to you* kind of attitude. And that can make people feel uncomfortable around you." Scripture says even a child is known by his actions. When a child is taught to greet others, to communicate, and to be mature, these skills automatically give them an open door to be more effective to build friendships and to encourage others spiritually.

Our parents have challenged us Duggars, whenever we're in a safe, social situation where our parents or older siblings are nearby, to look for the loneliest person in a room and go over and start up a conversation. This takes getting out of our comfort zone, but it is truly treating other people the way you would like to be treated. It's another thing that's a bit challenging to learn, and we're not saying it happens every time we're in a gathering where one person is sitting or standing alone, but it's something we try to remember to do.

We were also taught, when meeting people, to ask them questions about themselves. When we began doing that, we realized it's much easier to carry on conversations by purposely not asking a lot of questions that can be answered with a single word: "Yes," "No," "Fine." We practiced asking questions such as, "Have you lived here long?" "What town/area do you live in?" or, if it's a younger kid, "Where do you go to school?" or "Are you involved in any sports or do you play any musical instruments?" or "Do you attend a local church?"

Over the years we've built up a mental list of acceptable questions to ask to avoid that awkward silence that can result when people are getting acquainted. Of course, all of us have moments when we're tongue-tied and can't think of a thing to say, but when that happens, we know we can shoot up a little flare-prayer and God is always able to give us the words to say.

Since we were homeschooled and didn't have age-segregated classrooms, we've had good training grounds for learning to interact with all age groups. For the most part, we've all been pretty comfortable at a fairly early age carrying on conversations with adults. We love visiting with senior citizens and asking them questions about their family and their past work and life experiences. Dad has also instructed us on how, as young people, we should rise to our feet when shaking hands with an adult and always be looking for opportunities to open doors or give up our chair for our elders.

Mom also taught us telephone-answering skills when we were younger, and we practiced saying, "Hello, this is the Duggar residence, Jana speaking. How may I help you?" But now, because of the unique calls we get from all over the world, the house rule is that younger kids don't answer the phone.

Mom has said that *acceptance* is the sweetest language from one soul to another and that *rejection* is the most bitter. We have seen by her example that when you have a cheerful countenance and give an enthusiastic, friendly greeting to others over the phone or in person, the other persons feel God's love flowing through you to them in a special way. By investing in others' lives you quickly realize that the more you give of yourself, the more joy you receive! (Of course, our parents have cautioned us not to be too overly friendly with people of the opposite gender, as that can send the wrong kind of message!)

Duggar Family Hospitality

And now, on to one of our favorite topics: hospitality! Growing up, one of the biggest ways we practice putting communication skills and manners into action is when we welcome guests into our home for fellowship and a meal. Our house can require quite a bit of effort to get all cleaned up and organized beforehand, but we find that it's well worth it. I think we would all agree that some of our most wonderful memories are from those evenings when we've had other families in our home.

The Duggars can make a mess in a hurry, but when we all pitch in, we can clean up a place in no time flat. We divide up tasks, and everyone gets involved, from oldest to youngest. Some help prepare the meal while others clean up the house and yard. Having company is a good incentive to get organized, but Mom says if we waited until the house was spotless before we invited guests, we'd never have anyone over! If we don't have time to get everything done, we'll just focus on straightening up the downstairs and keep the upstairs-disaster-zone off-limits for the evening. But that's okay. We love the saying, "If you want to see us, stop by anytime. If you want to see the house, give us two weeks' notice!"

Another Duggar family tradition is that when we line up to fill our plates at mealtime, we let all guests go first, followed by the ladies in our family. The younger boys quite naturally want to zip to the front of the serving line. One day one of the boys, eager to chow down, came up with what seemed like a great idea to him (we will not mention his name, but it starts with the letter J). He

Pictured here (a few years ago) are Jill and Joy-Anna as they help prepare a meal in the kitchen.

simply filled his plate ahead of time while everyone else was lining up. Then he set it aside as he waited for the others to slowly make their way down the line. He was thinking he wouldn't have to risk being the last one in line, and as soon as the girls had their plates, he'd be all set to dig in. Jill explained to him that his idea was innovative but still impolite.

After sharing a meal together with guests, we usually have a time to play games together (chess, basketball, volleyball, foursquare, or the boys' favorite: football). Then, after most of the kids have run out their energy, Dad will usually call everyone to gather in the living room for Bible time and an opportunity to share testimonies and fellowship.

We always enjoy hearing salvation testimonies—how a person came to know the Lord and trust Him as Savior—and if we have a couple in our home, we almost always ask them to share how they met. Whether we are meeting new friends or spending time with old acquaintances, we continue to make such fond and wonderful memories together through these interactions.

From the time our parents were newly married and throughout our growing-up years, Mom and Dad have always gone out of their way to invest in others' lives. It seems like almost every week they are asked to counsel couples or to talk to a young person who is having some struggles. We all consider our home a ministry center that God has given us to use as a place where we can encourage others spiritually and enjoy special times of fellowship. We encourage other families to do the same, inviting a family to come for dinner and then direct the conversations to spiritual topics.

Many times our parents have guests over and then ask if it would be okay if we watch one of Jim Sammons's Financial Freedom Seminar messages together from embassyinstitute.org and then discuss it afterward. Once they watch one message, most people want to go through the whole series. Mom and Dad have used this to disciple others, and we all have seen many people grow in the Lord through this.

God desires for each person to experience a dynamic and abundant life. If we will ask Him to forgive us for the things we have done wrong and turn over the control of our lives to Him, He promises to freely give us eternal life! (Read John 3:16, 10:10, Romans 5:8, Ephesians 2:8,9.) The way you find true meaning in life is by discovering God's purpose in creating you. He wants to be your best friend, to put peace in your heart, and to lead you through life's journey.

THANK YOU FOR STICKING with us through this super-long chapter and letting us share some of the ideas involved in relating to the world while "growing up Duggar." We love sharing Jesus's love with others, along with the principles that have helped us in our own lives. Mom and Dad have modeled for us how to interact with others respectfully, how to share an enthusiastic greeting with all we meet, and the blessings of extending hospitality to people from all walks of life.

We know we've shared a *lot* of concepts about relationships, but it is our prayer that God will direct and encourage you as you begin to make them part of your own lives.

A FINAL WORD

Catch the Spark

THIS BOOK HAS BEEN written amid a great deal of prayer. As we've worked, we've thanked God for the opportunity to share our story, and we've asked Him to help this book become an encouragement to many other girls and to draw them closer to Him.

And again and again, we've prayed for *you*. We love you!

You are the reason we've written this book, and we've held you close to our hearts as we've worked. We hope by sharing our family's story, we've helped spark your enthusiasm for following Jesus.

From our heart to yours, we can tell you there is no greater purpose in life than knowing and having a real relationship with Jesus Christ. We pray that God will bless your life to the degree you seek to follow Him. We love you!

Jana, Jill, Jessa, and Jinger

Trust in the Lord with all thine heart;
and lean not unto thine own understanding.
In all thy ways acknowledge Him,
and He shall direct thy paths.
Be not wise in thine own eyes:
fear the LORD, and depart from evil.
—Proverbs 3:5–7

P.S. Please e-mail us at duggarmail@gmail.com and let us know how God is working in your lives.

Thank you for your interest in our family and for reading our story.
It's been a blessing to us to be able to share it with you.

ABOUT THE AUTHORS

Jana is the eldest of the Duggar daughters and finds joy in serving her family and others! She has enjoyed investing in the lives of young ladies through a ministry called "Journey to the Heart," which encourages young women in their relationship with God, their parents, their siblings, and others. A few years ago, she obtained her First Responders certification and in the past has volunteered on the local fire department. She has attended a number of births as a labor coach and stays busy managing the family mailroom when she is not traveling to share the love of Christ with others.

Jill has studied to become a midwife. She enjoys playing harp and violin, and studying Spanish. In 2013 she met Derick Dillard when he was serving in Nepal. Following their courtship and engagement, they were married in June 2014 and welcomed their son, Israel David, in May 2015. They are serving God internationally.

Jessa is talented at playing several instruments. She enjoys reading books, memorizing scripture, discipling friends, and spending time with her husband, Ben Seewald. They married in November 2014, had a special European honeymoon, and welcomed their first child,

Spurgeon Elliot, in November 2015. Future plans include outreach in their community, sharing the gospel of Jesus Christ, and adopting lots of children!

Jinger is always full of energy, that is, when she has a cup of coffee in her hand! She has become quite the photographer and likes picking up tips from professional crews that often come through. Jinger loves jammin' in the living room, playing duets on the piano with Jana. She has a passion to reach the world for Christ, so she often passes out gospel tracts in her many shopping outings!

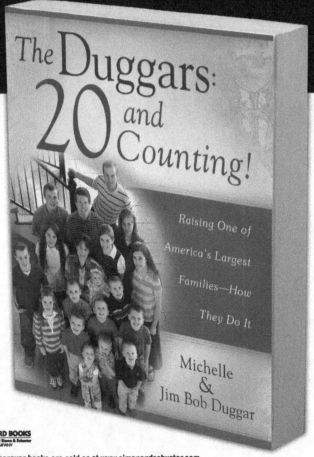